The Hot Dog Diaries
Stories from Morgantown's Oldest and Most Beloved Neighborhood Bar

Al Bonner
Jim Antonini

Pump Fake Press—Morgantown, WV
Paperback ISBN: 979-8-218-41033-9
eBook ISBN: 979-8-218-41034-6
Library of Congress Control Number: 2024909935
Title: *The Hot Dog Diaries: Stories from Morgantown's Oldest and Most Beloved Neighborhood Bar*
Author: Al Bonner & Jim Antonini
Digital distribution | 2024
Paperback | 2024

Front Cover: Photo by Ted Kisko; Stained glass by Mike Roh.

Back Cover: Clockwise from top, Owen Davis and the Free Hummus All Stars, pints of a Red Eye and Halleck Pale Ale, a famous Gene's hot dog, touring band The Dusty 45s from Seattle, Ryan Cain and the Ables, a typical order of hot dogs, Al Bonner–King of All Media, Gene's mural by Brian Pickens.

Dedication
By Al Bonner & Jim Antonini

This book is for everyone who has stepped through the front door of Gene's Beer Garden. Over the past eighty years, there have been too many beers and hot dogs consumed to count. But for all the beers poured and hot dogs prepared, there have been just as many laughs—probably more. Despite all the fun times, Gene's has lost many beloved regulars and bartenders through the years.

This book is dedicated to their memories and stories, so they and Gene's Beer Garden will live forever.

This book is also dedicated to the Perilli Family who opened Gene's Place in 1944.

Because of space limitations, the passage of time, and fading memories, it wasn't possible to include every funny or interesting story, or mention all those who have worked or regularly hung out at Gene's. We tried our best to come up with some good tales and memories we hope you will enjoy.

Table of Contents

Preface
By Al Bonner

"You know what you ought to do, Al?"

If I had a dollar for every time someone said that to me about Gene's, I'd be a millionaire. I've generally ignored or never got around to addressing all the suggestions over the years. But there have been so many people who have hung around Gene's since I've owned it and said, "There needs to be a book about the place."

So, here it is.

Introduction
By Al Bonner

This book wouldn't be complete without saying something about a man who meant so much to me. So many things have gone through my head as we put this book together. Memories that I'll carry with me for the rest of my life. Some happy, some sad, some that make you just shake your head and say, "No one's going to believe that!"

Over thirty-nine years ago, a man gave me an opportunity that completely changed my life forever. An opportunity that many wish for but never get the chance to make happen. That man was Frank Perilli. A tough, hardworking businessman who dedicated his life to taking care of his family. Many of you know who Frank was, but many may not.

On February 1st, 1985, I started my journey as the new owner of Gene's Beer Garden. It was cold. It was snowing. It was a lonely place as I sat there with only two customers chatting back and forth. One said, "You picked a great day to buy a bar, Al!" It seems so funny now. But shortly thereafter, the front door opened and in walked Frank.

"Come here, Al," he said, "and sit down with me. I want to talk to you."

I sat there for about an hour and listened to Frank share forty-one years of knowledge on how to run that place. He genuinely wanted me to succeed, and he took it upon himself to give me every opportunity to do so.

Up until that point, I only knew Frank as a hardworking businessman, willing to do whatever it took to support his family. It was ten hours a day, sweat on his upper lip, glasses sliding down his nose, hustling up and down the bar, pouring beers, and making hot dogs. Occasionally, he would flash a smile and let out a little laugh before going home at night to work on the books, pay the bills, and think about what needed to be done before the next morning.

Frank owed me nothing. I was twenty-eight years old and had somehow found a way into my dream. I had no clue what to do at that point but luckily there was Frank sitting with me and showing me the roadmap to success.

Did I follow the road the way he told me to take? No. Did I think there was an easier way? Yes. Was there? Absolutely not.

I made lots of mistakes. I didn't take care of the money.

"Put the money in the bank every day," he said. "Don't leave it in your pocket. There are holes in your pocket, and it won't be there when you need it."

It was during these times I found out Frank was more than just a tough businessman. He was a caring and compassionate man who truly did care about me and my success. He would say to me, "Al Bonner, you are a lucky man. You have a nice family. You take care of those little girls. That's what matters in life." Other than his family, I don't know if anyone else knew Frank that way.

I am a lucky man, Frank. You gave me a life-changing opportunity to own my dream. Thank you for giving me the opportunity to have you in my life. A friend, a mentor, and a man who was always willing to help me and wanted nothing more than for me to succeed.

I will miss you, Frank.

Chapter 1
Brief History of Gene's Beer Garden

Gene's as it appeared in the 1940's.

As of this writing, Gene's Place, or more commonly known by locals as Gene's Beer Garden, is eighty years old—the oldest bar in Morgantown, West Virginia. Morgantown is best known as the home to West Virginia University. Gene's was opened in 1944 by Gene Perilli in the Greenmont neighborhood, so his brothers, Frank and Joe, would have a place to work when they came back from the war. His sisters, Katie and Betty, worked at the bar as well. The Perillis owned Gene's until 1985 when the business was purchased by Al Bonner. The bar has always had a simple food menu of hot dogs, barbeque sandwiches, cheese plates, and snacks, such as pretzels and potato chips. Later after Al had purchased the bar, he added pepperoni rolls to the menu.

Early Gene's menu board.

Over several months in 2023 and 2024, Al sat down with me (Jim Antonini) and, over beers, recounted the history of the neighborhood bar and told me some of the many, many stories that *are* Gene's Beer Garden, as much as the photographs, newspaper articles, flyers that promote or memorialize important events, cartoons, letters from patrons—all the mementos that cover the walls of the rooms that make up Gene's.

During its entire existence, Gene's has served as a gathering place for the neighborhood and Morgantown community. For decades, it would open early in the morning and serve coal miners after they got off the midnight shift. During the time the Perilli family owned the bar, Gene had a barber shop, first in the basement, then in the back room, where he cut hair for many years. It was a popular place for the families of the neighborhood to bring their kids for their haircuts. As the kids waited in the back room to get their hair cut, their parents would be at the bar, enjoying hot dogs and pints of beer. More recently, a barber shop again opened in the back of Gene's, appropriately named Gene's Hair Garden.

In the early days, there were bocce ball courts where the parking lot is currently located. Bocce ball was extremely popular then with the many Italian immigrant families who lived in the neighborhood at the time. Later, pinball machines, a jukebox, pool tables, dart boards, poker machines, and large screen televisions would be added to entertain the patrons.

Bartender Josh Graham at the pool table in the basement of Gene's. Photo by Ted Kisko.

Since Al has owned Gene's, the bar has hosted all types of celebrations. There have been parties for birthdays, retirements, and graduations. There have been wedding receptions and bridal and baby showers. There has been at least one wedding and one funeral. The wedding took place behind Gene's in the parking lot, where the bocce ball courts used to be, and the funeral took place in the back room of the bar. An actual embalmed body was carried into Gene's and placed on the long table in back for the viewing and memorial service.

A stage was built in the early 2000s to accommodate local and touring musicians. Gene's now has a speakeasy bar in the basement that can be rented for private parties and events. The speakeasy was built with generous help from a group of loyal friends, customers, and employees. Most of the work was done during the *Covid* pandemic, when Gene's, like all the other bars and restaurants in the area, was shut down for an extended period.

Left, Gene's speakeasy. Right, members of the team that constructed the speakeasy in 2020.

The beer selection was limited for the first several decades after Gene's opened. There originally was a choice of only one or two types of draft beer and a handful of bottle and can selections. When Al purchased Gene's, he had three beer taps: Busch, Busch, and Busch. When one keg of Busch kicked, he would move to the next one. Now, in Gene's eightieth year of operation, there is a wide selection of all styles of beers, from stouts to porters and pale ales, from sours to ciders to pilsners and lagers. Today, Gene's has a selection of sixteen different beers on tap with nearly fifty other choices in bottles and cans, many from local breweries.

Left, bartender Tarik Kalwar pours a draft. Right, view of the bar. Photos by Ted Kisko.

But Gene's Beer Garden is more than a place to get something to eat, have a beer, or watch a ball game. It's a place to gather with friends — to see a familiar face, to share a laugh, to be included.

Everyone has always been welcomed at Gene's. Greenmont is the most diverse neighborhood in Morgantown and that is reflected in the clientele who visit Gene's daily. Many of the folks who regularly hang out at Gene's are closer to each other than their own families. And it's been that way for eighty years.

Longtime and former bartender, Shey Schuetzner said it best: "There is no other bar like Gene's. It's a family."

The outside of Gene's today. Photo by Ted Kisko.

Chapter 2
Peanut Versus the World

"**H**ey Al, how many times have you fired Peanut?"

"At least ten times, probably more."

Peanut was Gene's longest-working bartender since Al bought the bar. He could be grumpy and impatient. He was always ornery but also lovable. He and Al were best friends. He would gamble on anything—the daily numbers, dogs and horses, cards, and video poker. He spent his free time in dive bars around Morgantown, and in Point Marion and Mount Morris across the state line in Pennsylvania. He would often be late for work or not show up at all. And he loved the women—all ages and all sizes.

While bartending one night, he was hitting on two young women at the bar. It was late, near closing. He had been drinking—a lot. He didn't know that the two ladies had zero interest in him or any other man. They were together, a couple. But Peanut kept trying. He left the bar open for them well past closing time, hoping to get some action from one or both. Eventually, they were gone. Now quite drunk and alone, Peanut attempted to take the money tray from the cash register to the safe in back but only made it as far as the second booth in the front room. After stumbling into the booth, he passed out with the cash tray full of money beside him. All the lights in the bar were turned on, and the front door was unlocked.

Al's dad, who at the time made chili and cut onions for the bar, came into Gene's at his usual early time of 6 AM in the morning. He noted the drunk man in the booth, not realizing it was Peanut. He prepped the food for two hours in the kitchen in back, allowing the man more time to sleep.

Using the phone behind the bar, he finally called Al at 8 AM.

"Al, you got a drunk passed out in a booth here. The lights were on, and the door was unlocked when I got here."

"Who is it?" Al asked.

"I don't know. He has his head down in his arms."

"Check who it is," Al said.

Just then, Peanut was awakened by Al's dad on the phone and raised his head. Al's dad glanced at the booth and saw Peanut staring at him.

"It's Peanut."

"I'll be right up," Al said.

But before Al got there, Peanut grabbed handfuls of $20 bills from the cash tray, stuffed them in his pockets, and dashed away. Nobody saw him for weeks.

xxx

"It's busy as hell in the bar," Al remembered. "I think it was a WVU football Saturday. We were out of plastic cups. Peanut was bartending. I was helping him. I gave him $20 to run to the store to grab a bag of plastic cups. Several of the regulars at the bar also gave him money to buy them cigarettes. He never came back. It was a Friday almost a month later when he walked back into the bar. He showed up with five cups and gave me $3 in change. I swore I would never hire him again."

"But you did," said someone at the bar who

9

had been listening.

"I needed someone to work the next day, a WVU home football game. None of the other bartenders wanted to work on game days. They wanted to go to the games. So, he was behind the bar the very next day."

xxx

On another occasion, Peanut was late for work. Al was behind the bar, getting restless. He had already fired Peanut a couple of times that year. He didn't know Peanut had been pulled over in the Sabraton neighborhood on his way to work. He had an expired inspection sticker and tags on his license plate.

It turned out the cop who pulled him over was the same cop who had pulled him over for the same reason weeks before. He also knew Peanut from Gene's. The cop let him off with a second warning.

"If I catch you in this blue car again with expired stickers, I'm taking your ass directly to jail."

After the cop left, Peanut sped to Gene's and drove up Wilson Avenue.

"There he is," one of the regulars at Gene's said from his barstool, staring out the window as Peanut went right past the bar. "And there he goes."

Peanut took a right to the parking lot behind Gene's. He parked and disappeared on foot down

Green Street. Al walked around back to the parking lot, looking for him. Peanut didn't return until thirty minutes later, carrying a can of black house paint and a paint brush roller.

"What in the hell are you doing?" Al asked him.

"Not going to jail," Peanut said as he rolled the thick paint on the old blue car in hopes of camouflaging it.

"How'd it look when he was finished?" someone at the bar asked.

"It looked pretty good." Al grinned.

xxx

It had been a tough year for several of the bar regulars for a variety of reasons. It was New Year's Day sometime in the 1990s. Peanut was bartending.

"It's been a pretty shitty year," bar regular Owen Davis lamented. "My girlfriend left me. She took the dog with her. I'm looking forward to the start of a new one."

"Hell, it's been a great year for me," Peanut chimed in. "I only had one heart attack and no divorces."

xxx

Not many people knew what Peanut's real name was. One time while working at the bar, he was having severe chest pains. Two of the regulars,

11

Roadie and Ed Row, took him to the hospital emergency room. Peanut was admitted and taken to a room in the back for tests. Ed and Roadie waited for him in the busy waiting room. Every fifteen or twenty minutes, a nurse would come into the waiting room and call out, "Are the folks who brought in Blaine Forman here?"

This went on for a couple hours as Ed and Roadie waited.

"Are the folks who brought in Blaine Forman here?" the nurse asked again.

Ed looked to Roadie and said, "I feel bad for that Blaine Forman guy. Seems like his people just dumped him off and left."

The nurse again entered the waiting room many minutes later, "Are the two men who brought Blaine Forman in here?"

Roadie glanced to Ed and asked, "Hey, wait a minute, what's Peanut's real name?"

xxx

On a trip to New Orleans, Al noted how many of the popular bars there had bartenders who cheerfully greeted all the folks who entered, "Welcome to the Erin Rose!"

"When I get back to Morgantown," he said. "I'm going to have my bartenders say, 'Welcome to Gene's!' whenever someone comes in."

On his first night back in town, Al sat at the bar and pointed to the front door, telling Peanut,

"Whenever someone walks through that door you have to say, 'Welcome to Gene's!'"

Peanut stared at Al with a blank, almost annoyed, look. The door to the bar suddenly opened. A young couple walked in. Al looked at Peanut and motioned to the couple who had just entered.

"Fuck you, Al," Peanut muttered with a slight shake of his head as he walked to the other side of the bar.

xxx

An older gentleman entered Gene's. He studied the place for a moment before approaching the bar. It was obvious he had never been there before. Peanut was working. Al was sitting at the end of the bar.

"Can I help you?" Peanut asked the man.

"A draft of Bud," the man said.

Peanut handed him the frosty pint of beer.

"Are you Gene?" the man naively asked Peanut.

Peanut pointed to Al who glanced at the stranger.

"Are you Gene's father?" the man innocently asked Peanut.

Al busted out laughing as Peanut, who looked significantly older than Al, shook his head and walked away from the man.

"What's so funny?" the stranger asked Al.

"He's only a few years older than me."

The man's face turned bright red as Peanut disappeared to the video poker room in the back.

xxx

Al was home one evening and heard a knocking at his door. It was Peanut.

"Can I use your bathroom?" he asked.

"Yeah, I suppose," Al said, pointing down the hallway.

Peanut entered the bathroom and locked the door. After a few minutes, Al could hear water from the shower running. After about fifteen minutes, Peanut came out of the bathroom. He had one of Al's bath towels rolled up under his arm. It was wet. Al stared at Peanut who walked to the front door. Peanut stopped before leaving and turned.

"Can I borrow fifty bucks?"

Al reached into his pocket, pulled out $50, and handed it to him without asking any questions. Peanut left with the wet towel and the money.

After about a week, there was a knock on the front door of Al's house. It was Peanut. He didn't say a word as he gave Al his towel back and the $50 he had borrowed.

Months later, Al asked him why he needed to shower in his bathroom.

"It was a rough morning," he said. "I had just shit my pants."

Peanut started dating a woman named Cathy who had been hanging out at Gene's. She was a member of The Way religious group. Many at the bar thought she was only there attempting to convert them from a so-called wasted life of drinking and smoking in a bar to a more spiritual life.

"You better be careful, Peanut," Al warned. "She may brainwash you and get you to join her cult."

"She better watch out," Peanut snapped back. "Or she may end up worshipping at the Church of Peanut."

Peanut and Cathy were inseparable for days. He was supposed to work one afternoon but was late. Al was furious. As Al worked in his place, the phone at the bar rang. It was the owner of Horton Ford car dealership in Sabraton.

"Have you seen Peanut?" he asked Al over the phone.

"No," Al said. "He's supposed to be here working but never showed up."

"He took a brand-new Ford Mustang for a test drive earlier today and never brought it back."

"I'll try to find him and call you," Al said.

Earlier that day, Peanut wanted to impress Cathy. He knew the owner of Horton Ford left the dealership daily at noon to go to lunch. Peanut showed up at the dealership a few minutes after noon. He approached a young car salesman and told him he was friends with the owner, who said he could take one of the new Mustangs for a test drive. The salesman got Peanut the keys.

Peanut picked up Cathy in the brand-new car and took her to Point Marion, Pennsylvania, where they proceeded to barhop at all his favorite joints—The Brass Rail and The Eagles Club, among others. Sometime in the early evening, they ended up at his mom's house in Morgantown. She was in Florida on vacation. Both Peanut and Cathy were quite drunk and passed out in his mom's bed together. He forgot about working at Gene's and about returning the Mustang to the car dealer. Worried, Al had searched for him at all his favorite local bars into the evening but kept missing him. He even drove to Point Marion. He never found Peanut.

When Al returned to Gene's, the owner of the car dealer called back.

"If Peanut doesn't return that car by nine tonight," he threatened, "I'll have to report it to the police as stolen."

Sometime after midnight, Peanut woke up to use the bathroom. He looked out the bedroom window of his mother's house and saw the Mustang.

"Shit!"

He hustled out of the house and sped back to the car dealer's lot. He circled the lot several times and found an open spot between two cars in the rear of the place near a service entrance. Then he walked three and half miles back to his mother's place. He crawled into bed and snuggled up to Cathy's naked rear end. She didn't even know he'd been gone.

He awoke the next day to pounding on the front door of his mother's house. It was the deputy sheriff. He and a group of city policemen came to ask him about the Mustang.

"I returned it yesterday afternoon like I promised," Peanut lied, telling the deputy sheriff where the Mustang was parked. "And tell old man Shearer I don't think I want to do it. I wasn't impressed."

xxx

Peanut was working. Big Bob Hamilton, a future regular of Gene's, had come into the bar for the first time. He had never met Peanut before. Bob sat at an open stool and placed his ball cap on the bar. It was a very hot July afternoon. He was excessively perspiring as he quickly drained a couple of beers. Peanut approached to pour him another one.

"It's hot in here," Bob said to Peanut. "Can you turn up the air conditioning?"

Annoyed, Peanut stared at the newcomer a moment before grabbing his ball cap from the bar. Puzzled, Bob studied Peanut, who took the cap and dunked it in the cold water in the sink.

17

Peanut then reached over the bar and, to the shock of everyone there, slapped the sopping wet hat onto Bob's sweaty head.

"There," Peanut growled. "Is that better?"

Bob just laughed and laughed. He and Peanut would become fast friends. No one could annoy Peanut more than Bob Hamilton. He always paid with checks and asked for cash back, usually in obscure amounts that required change in pennies—and it had been decades since Gene's had pennies in the cash register. There hadn't been pennies in the register since bar regular John Barnes paid for an afternoon of beers with pennies he had collected in a large Mason jar. Tarik Kalwar, the bartender at the time, was not too happy with Barnes.

xxx

Peanut was very sick. He had cancer. He was nearly blind. He hadn't worked at the bar for a couple of years. Knowing Peanut's days on earth were likely numbered, Al and three of Gene's bartenders went to his apartment to visit him. Lucy Morrison, Steve Brady, and Tarik arrived in the early afternoon with Al.

"This guy was dying," Tarik remembered. "He couldn't see. He was in horrible pain. But his place was spotless. He had a cat, and it didn't smell like a litter box. He was well-groomed, and his clothes were clean and pressed. And he was dying. He was

18

still taking care of himself and the place."

"We all joined him at the kitchen table," Tarik went on. "It was a little uncomfortable at first. We all were thinking this might be the last time we would see him. I had trouble looking him in the eyes. We all did. He lit a cigarette and took several deep breaths off it. The first few minutes were nothing but awkward small talk. Finally, Peanut broke the ice."

"Raise your hand if you got a blowjob today," Tarik recalled Peanut saying to their surprise. "We all looked at each other and shrugged, half-grinning. Peanut calmly placed his cigarette in the ashtray, before raising his hand high in the air. We all busted out laughing. I thought Lucy was going to lose her shit. Eventually, Peanut started laughing. His hand was still in the air."

"He would pass away a week later," Tarik continued after a short pause. "I loved that man."

Al with Peanuts shortly before his death.

Chapter 3
Snow Days

"You know what you ought to do, Al?"
"What?"
"Buy a snowblower."

Snowman outside of Gene's. Photo by Lucy Morrison.

It was one of those historical snowfalls in Morgantown; twenty-eight inches of snow had fallen over the course of one night. The town was shut down. Everything was closed: the city offices, the county schools, the university classes, and most of the businesses in the area except for a couple of convenience stores. But like always, Gene's was open. Gene's never closed no matter how much snow had piled up.

To open for business, Al would have to shovel the sidewalk and steps in front of the bar after heavy snowfalls. Oftentimes, he would do it alone. Many times, it would take hours and a lot of sweat and hard work to remove all the snow. He always cleared the sidewalks using just a snow shovel. After this particular snowstorm, it took him nearly three hours to remove the snow. He shoveled it from the sidewalk into large piles that lined Wilson Avenue for nearly a hundred feet in front of his bar.

When finished, he stood on the cleared sidewalk, sweating and trying to catch his breath as he admired his completed hard work. Within minutes, one of the bar regulars, Pat Brezito, came barreling up Wilson in his pick-up truck. He had a snowplow he would attach to the front end of the truck to clear driveways and parking lots of different businesses around town for extra cash. As he approached Gene's, he angled the plow in the direction of the bar and lowered it. There were no cars parked out front. The plow on the truck struck the deep mounds of shoveled snow in front of Gene's, blowing it high in the air. Within seconds, the sidewalk, the steps, the front window of the bar, and Al were covered in several inches of snow — three hours of work wasted. Laughing hysterically, Pat sped away.

With his snow shovel in his hand, Al rushed to his truck and chased Pat to his house, following him for several blocks through the neighborhood. Pat parked in his driveway and quickly disappeared inside, locking the front door. He knew Al was enraged. In his haste, Pat forgot to lock his truck. Al parked in the driveway behind Pat's truck. He grabbed his shovel and opened the front door to Pat's truck. For the next ten minutes, Al furiously shoveled piles of snow into the cab of Pat's truck, filling it. Al slammed the front door to the truck and laughed all the way back to Gene's.

"You got me good, Al," Pat said after returning to Gene's the next day. "You got me good."

After that, Al usually made Joe Lucas, a regular and sometime employee at the bar, shovel the sidewalks after heavy snowfalls.

To this day, Pat claims it was a mistake. He thought he had angled the plow in the opposite direction.

Pat Brezito climbing the walls of Gene's.

xxx

After a different large snowfall, Al not only spent most of the day shoveling the sidewalk in front of the bar, he also cleared the parking spots on Wilson Street in front with a shovel so the bar patrons would have clear places to park.

A young lady who lived in the neighborhood happened to park in one of the cleared spots as the places in front of her apartment were blocked by mounds of plowed snow. Quite tipsy and a little ornery after a full snow day of drinking beer, several of the bar regulars, who will not be named, weren't too happy the young woman took one of the valuable open spots on the street.

In no time, the regulars each grabbed a shovel and frantically started to cover her car in snow, completely burying it. To make matters worse, they formed an assembly line, passing pitchers of water from inside to the outside of the bar. The last guy at the end of the line outside would pour the water over the snow-covered car. With temperatures hovering near zero, the car soon was encased in a block of ice.

The fun quickly ended as the young lady returned to her car. The regulars giggled as they watched from the bar's front window. Her jaw nearly dropped from her mouth. She angrily stomped into the bar and wanted to know who had buried the car. She needed to go to work. The bartender and regulars at the bar just shrugged. She hurriedly returned to her apartment and called the police. A city police officer eventually arrived at Gene's. Exhausted, he was in no mood for games. He had spent most of the day in the frigid weather helping stranded motorists stuck in ditches or investigating numerous fender benders caused by the icy roads.

Like the young woman, he asked who covered the car in snow. Everybody just shook their heads and shrugged. He stared down each of the shit-faced bar regulars for many minutes, looking for one to break. None did. He glanced at the bartender.

"I'll be back," the cop said. "I want this car cleaned off as soon as possible. And if it's not by the time I come back, I'm shutting this place down and dragging all your asses to jail."

After the police officer left, the guys in the bar hopped off their barstools and rushed to clear the car. After that night, no one ever talked about that incident again.

xxx

Snowy day at Gene's. Photo by Ted Kisko.

A blizzard had shut down all of Morgantown and the entire surrounding area. The interstates all were closed. Two of Gene's regulars, Brian Reed and Kevin Murphy, were stuck in Grafton, in Tucker County, approximately fifty miles from Morgantown. The sun was starting to set.

25

Needing a beer and afraid they were missing the raucous snow day celebration at Gene's with their friends, they filled a snowmobile that belonged to Brian's dad with gas and hopped on. They sliced through the mounds of snow on several nearly impassable backroads to the closed Interstate 79.

Without hesitation, Brian gunned the snowmobile towards an interstate merge point, causing it to fishtail as they pulled onto the empty snow-covered highway and headed north. With their goggle-covered faces blanketed in fresh snow, they laughed so hard they nearly lost their breath in the frigid air as Brian pushed the roaring snow machine to its maximum speed. They raced the setting sun alone on the interstate for what seemed like eternity. Pushed to its limit, the speeding snowmobile violently rattled as it bounced over deep drifts of snow that had settled on the highway. Brian held on to the grips of the handlebars so tightly his hands grew numb. Kevin nearly bounced off the back several times as he bearhugged Brian's chest, squeezing the air out of him. They had never felt such a thrill in their lives.

It wasn't until they passed Fairmont and neared Morgantown that the snowmobile encountered other vehicles on the interstate. They passed a few snowplows and salt trucks that tried to keep ahead of the quickly falling snow, rushing to clear the covered roadway. The snowmobile skated by a couple of state police cars stationed at the ends of the interstate on-ramps, blocking other vehicles from entering the closed highway. One of the policemen even hit the blue lights of his car and started to enter the interstate as if he were about to give chase. But wisely, he stopped, knowing he was no match for the speeding snow machine on its mad and wild dash to Gene's. Kevin claimed he raised his right arm and flipped the state policeman his middle finger as the snowmobile disappeared into the snowy winter night.

Several of the bar regulars happened to be standing outside of Gene's smoking cigarettes and enjoying pints of beers in the falling snow when they heard an obnoxiously loud revving sound roaring towards them. In no time, Brian and Kevin barreled up Wilson Avenue on the racing snowmobile towards the group. Recognizing Brian and Kevin, the Gene's regulars began to cheer before wildly laughing. Miscalculating the distance he needed to stop and the high rate of speed that the snow machine was traveling, Brian steered the snowmobile towards the entrance of Gene's, tightly gripping the hand brakes. The snowmobile skidded over the icy roadway and aggressively struck a small snowbank that lined the sidewalk in front of the bar, sending the snowmobile into the air. It smashed into the front brick wall of the building, shattering its plastic front end into pieces.

"I swear," Al remembered. "The entire building shook from the impact. They were lucky they weren't thrown through the window."

Chapter 4
More Than Just World Class Hot Dogs

"**H**ey Al, how many hot dogs do you think you've eaten here at Gene's?" someone at the bar asked.

"Well, if I averaged one a day since I've owned the place, I would say about 14,000 hot dogs."

xxx

The world-famous Gene's hot dog—the most popular food item at the bar

When ordered with everything, it originally was served with only chili sauce, mustard, and onions on it. If someone wanted ketchup, they had to pay an extra five cents. Now, a variety of additional toppings are available, including coleslaw, cheese, relish, and different hot sauces.

xxx

The Gene's pepperoni roll — the second most popular food item at the bar

For those who didn't grow up in West Virginia and don't know, the pepperoni roll was originally conceived of as part of lunch for coal miners. It is basically a bread roll with pepperoni baked inside of it. They were perfect for lunch in the mines as they are easily packed in a lunch pail, didn't need to be refrigerated, and could be eaten by hand like a sandwich. They are readily available in convenience stores, gas stations, lunch counters, and bars throughout West Virginia. Anything that can be added to a hot dog can be added to a pepperoni roll.

xxx

The infamous and all-mighty Gene's supreme

A recent photo of Shey Schuetzner holding her creation–the Gene's Supreme. Photo Jenny Roberts.

It began as a joke and became a popular but secret menu item — not everyone knew about it at first.

Although the most talked about and curious food item available at Gene's, it is universally hated by bartenders who have been asked to make one. In one sandwich, it contains just about every food Gene's has to offer.

It is not on the menu. You must ask for it. But beware, the bartender may refuse to make it if they are too busy or don't know the person ordering it. It takes some time and effort to put it together. It always seems to be ordered when the bartender is at their busiest.

The Gene's Supreme was created sometime in the late 1990s by former bartender Shey Schuetzner. She was working at the bar and concerned about Charles Randolph, another bartender at the time, who had been on quite a bender.

"Charles," Shey said, "you need to eat. What do you want? I'll make you anything."

"I'll take one of everything," Charles said, being difficult.

"Come on, Charles. What do you want?"

"I want one of everything."

"What do you want? A hot dog? A pepperoni roll? Barbeque?"

"Yeah," he mumbled. "All that."

"Okay," she said.

She cut open a pepperoni roll long ways and stuffed it with onions and slices of white American cheese. She put the stuffed roll into the microwave for a short time. After melting the cheese and warming the bun, she added a hot dog wiener inside it and covered it with chili sauce, a spoonful of barbeque, and cole slaw. She coated the messy creation with ketchup, mustard, and Frank's hot sauce, before topping it off with a fistful of crumbled potato chips. She got the idea for the last part from something her mother did when she was young. Her mother used to sprinkle crushed potato chips on tops of chicken and rice casseroles after they came out of the oven.

Lucy Morrison, the longest-tenured current Gene's bartender, was intently listening as Shey recalled the story of the first Gene's Supreme.

"You, know," Lucy spoke up, half-laughing. "I had to make seventeen of those fuckers one time."

"How many?"

"It was during a shift change. The worst time possible time. Shannon was coming in after me. Ah, I had a bitch of a day. I just wanted to get out of there. The Hash Harriers. The running club in town suddenly came in. They were all sweaty and loud, singing songs. They were a big group, led by Tim Nelms. He ordered seventeen of those bastards. Shannon had never made one before, so I had to stay and help her. I was there another hour."

"Was Tim wearing any pants?" asked Jenny Robers who had been listening to the story. (Author's note: Tim Nelms is a retired MD and celebrated exhibitionist and naturalist who sometimes liked to prance around specific bars in town naked.)

"Yeah, he was!" Lucy said and laughed. "If he hadn't been, I would've cut off *his* wiener and used it on his own personal Gene's Supreme!"

xxx

The Gene's cheese plate—the most ridiculed food item available at the bar

A cheese plate with yellow mustard by Christy Jacobs. Photo by Bevin Van Gilder.

It is basically several thick slices of mild cheddar cheese served on a paper hot dog wrapper with yellow mustard. It was so popular with one young man who lived in an apartment across the street he was given the nickname 'Cheese Plate' by the bar regulars. Having been on house arrest for a year, Cheese Plate wore an ankle bracelet, but when he stood at the bar in Gene's he was still close enough to his apartment that the bracelet's signal wasn't triggered. Not having many options for food outside his apartment, he would be seen in Gene's multiple times a day, ordering cheese plates.

"Food recommendations: I eat my hot dog with chili, slaw, ketchup, and onion. The chili-cheese pepperoni roll is some of the best drunk food of all time. Warning: *DO NOT GET THE CHEESE PLATE.*"

Gene's Beer Garden, YELP Review: Ryan N.,
Washington, DC.
February 22, 2009

xxx

The Gene's red eye — a drink so good a song was written about it

"A beautiful concoction/fit for consumption/For breakfast, lunch, or dinner, it's always a winner/Make mine a RED EYE!"

— Lyrics to "Red Eye" by Owen Davis
from *Among the Teeming Millions*, 1994.

A red eye is an icy mug, 2/3 filled with cold domestic draft and 1/3 with chilled tomato juice. It's good for early morning hangovers as well as the final beer of the night at last call. A good red eye has been known to replenish the soul.

> "Let's go to Gene's for red eyes to sober up. Red eyes ain't drinking."
> — Dave Davis, Owen's brother

xxx

No shirt, no shoes — no service!

The state health inspector was at Gene's one morning sometime in the 1990s. He came out of the kitchen to the bar in front. Al's dad was in the back, chopping onions and making chili like he did.

"Did you know the fellow in back cutting onions is not wearing a shirt?" the inspector said to Al, who was tending bar.

"Yeah, that's my dad. He takes his shirt off before he starts the food prep," Al answered with a shrug. "He doesn't want it to smell like onions."

"He can't do that." The inspector shook his head.

"I know, I know. I'll tell him."

When Al arrived at Gene's the next day, he walked back to the kitchen to check on his dad. He again had his shirt off, but he also wore an apron over his bare chest. The apron happened to be a see-through clear plastic one he had found at the bar. It had a large martini glass with an olive in it on the front.

"He looked ridiculous," Al remembered.

xxx

A reason to live above the bar

Gene's at night. Photo by Ted Kisko.

Bar regular and local musician, Jeff Wiles, had been working with his father, renovating the bathroom of a small house he owned. After a hard day of work, they went to Gene's to grab a bite to eat and a cold beer. It was one of the first times Jeff's father, Howard, had been to Gene's.

It was a warm Spring evening. The sun was setting. The windows of the bar were open. A pleasant breeze blew through the place. As they enjoyed chili hot dogs and pints of beer, Howard soaked in the pleasant vibe and cozy atmosphere of Gene's. Neither said a word for many minutes. Finally, Howard broke the ice, knowing there were apartments above the bar.

"You know, son, ideally you'd live upstairs of this place."

xxx

This isn't Texas Roadhouse

Al decided to provide free peanuts at the bar. The free peanuts, still in shells, were placed throughout Gene's in several plastic bowls. He did it for two reasons. One, he thought it would be nice to offer a free snack to his customers. And two, he thought the salty nuts would increase beer consumption, and increased beer consumption would equal increased beer sales. But he quickly discovered the free snack idea was a mistake — a huge mistake. He didn't account for the mess of empty peanut shells and skins left behind.

Two of Gene's most mischievous regulars, Roadie and Huey Nieman, would save the piles of empty peanut shells in bags. When Al was not around, they would unscrew the tops of the barstools, remove the barstool seats, and fill the barstool hollow metal posts with the empty shells.

"It was pain in the ass to clean the posts out," Al remembered. "We'd have to vacuum them out with a hose. I had to get the shells out of there. I didn't need them attracting mice or cockroaches."

"I was about ready to kick them out of the bar," Al continued. "Then I got an idea. I started saving the shells myself. I probably had a large plastic garbage bag full of them. One morning, Huey and Gary Davies were in the bar. Dave Anderson and I snuck out back and got into Huey's car. They were about to go on a short road trip. I stuffed probably five pounds of empty shells into his glovebox. It was so full, me and Dave had to push with all our weight against it to close it shut. With shells I had left, I stuffed handfuls of them above both sun visors."

Al then came back into the bar. After a couple of hot dogs and beers, Huey and Gary left Gene's. Al couldn't help but laugh. One of the regulars asked what he was laughing about.

"You'll see," Al said.

In a matter of minutes, Huey and Gary stepped back into Gene's. They both were covered in pieces of spent peanut shells. They had shells in their hair, on their faces, in their mouths, and all over the fronts of their shirts. It looked as if they were shot from close range with a shotgun filled with peanuts shells.

"That was a good one, Al," Huey said, spitting pieces of peanut shells from his mouth.

"I knew you'd be back," Al said with a laugh.

"We turned onto Brockway and hit a bump," Huey said. "The glovebox blew open. It was like a bomb went off. I nearly wrecked us. I guess we're even now."

"Have a good trip," Al said, still laughing as Huey and Gary left the bar again.

After returning to the car, Huey and Gary each closed their door at the same time. As the doors slammed shut, both sun visors flipped down, pouring the empty peanut shells onto their heads. Huey claimed it was years before he even got rid of all shells from his car.

Chapter 5
Bartenders, Regulars, And Mischief

I'll have a Betty

In the 1990s, long-time regular Betty Hilliard used to ask for half pours of beer before leaving to go home. A "Betty" became popular through the years with regulars who needed to go home but weren't quite ready to leave the bar. Most times, one Betty would turn into several Betty beers. Her legacy lives on not only at Gene's but at other bars in Morgantown where the order of a Betty is understood to be a half-pour of beer.

Betty used to cover her glass of beer with a napkin. People would ask her why. She claimed it kept the "beer gnats" away.

Betty and Peanut had a short but steamy affair years ago. Betty would say, "Peanut was the only man who ever knocked my socks off. I needed my oxygen tank after we would finish."

xxx

The matriarch of Gene's

Right, Lucy behind the bar. Left, Recording of the *Everyone Loves Lucy* Gene's podcast.

These days most people associate Gene's with Lucy Morrison. She has been a muti-year winner of Best Bartender in town as named by

Morgantown Magazine. Her daily goal is to make everyone who enters the bar feel welcomed, whether it's their first or hundredth time there. She moved to the United States from Ireland twenty-six years ago. She has worked at Gene's for twenty-three of those years—the longest tenured bartender besides Peanut since Al has owned the bar. When we asked folks who frequent Gene's about Lucy, first their faces lit up, then a series of common responses were given:

"She makes the place feel comfortable."

"It feels like home when I walk in and see her."

"She treats me like family."

Lucy claims the only person she ever threw out of the bar was Christopher, her brother, who she threw out twice.

According to Al, "Where's Lucy?" is the most-asked question at the bar if she isn't there. During shift changes with Lucy, current bartender Josh Graham says she tells him every time before leaving, "Have a good shift. I love you. And don't take bullshit from anyone."

When Lucy started bartending at Gene's, she technically wasn't allowed to work due to her immigration status at the time. Also, at that time, Al was late in returning his beer license renewal for the bar. He wasn't legally supposed to open Gene's until it arrived, which he was told would be any day. But he opened the bar anyway.

Vic Cordwell, Jamie W., and two or three

others were quite intoxicated, and it wasn't even 10 AM yet. As Al was driving to Gene's that morning, he spotted two state police cars parked in front of his bar. He expected the worst.

"Oh, shit," he remembered. "They are going to shut me down for good. My bar had no license, and my bartender was an illegal alien. Lucy's Irish accent is kind of obvious, you know."

As he was parking, his phone rang. It was J. R. Kiger, a regular who resembled Dan Ackroyd. He helped Al in the mornings with kitchen prep work. J. R. was the nervous type.

"Al," he whispered into the phone while hunkered down in the kitchen. "You better get here."

"I just pulled up. What's goin' on?"

"The Governor's here."

"Governor? What Governor?"

"The Governor of West Virginia."

"What's he want?"

"I don't know."

"You don't know?"

"I'm hiding in the back."

"Jesus Christ! I'll be in!"

Al anxiously hurried into the bar. He was greeted by Charlene Marshall, the Mayor of Morgantown, and Bob Wise, the Governor of West Virginia, as well as two hulking state troopers who were acting as his bodyguards. It seemed the Governor was touring different neighborhoods around the state. It was part of an outreach program his office had developed to improve neighborhood safety. Charlene was giving him a tour of the Greenmont neighborhood.

Both drunk, Vic and Jamie were engaged in playful banter with the Governor. He had given them each a brochure that described his program. There was a photograph of the Governor on the brochure that appeared to have been taken years before, when he was younger. Without warning, Jamie reached over and yanked the hat the Governor was wearing off his head. The Governor and his state trooper bodyguards seemed more confused than threatened by Jamie's aggressive action. Jamie studied the photo in the brochure and glanced at the Governor.

"You had more hair in this picture," he said, "and probably more balls back then as well."

"Now you did it," Vic slurred to Jamie, motioning to the Governor. "If I'm about to be executed with a lethal injection by the State, and there's only one person in this world who could save me, you jus' pissed him off."

"We'll be back for lunch," the Mayor spoke up, trying whisk the Governor out of Gene's. "I told him about how great the chili dogs you have here."

As she started to lead the somewhat distracted Governor from the bar, he grabbed his hat from Jamie and slammed it on his head.

"Quick!" Al suddenly said to Lucy after the Mayor and Governor left. "Lock the door! Gene's is closed until I get my license!"

xxx

Jingle balls

It was a Gene's Christmas party sometime in the early 2000s. Joe Lucas was the first to go through the potluck buffet line of food brought in by the regulars in the back room of the bar and fill his plate. He found an open seat near the end of the table where the food line ended. Holding the heaping plate of food out in front of him, he started to eat. His legs were wide open, spread eagle-like, for all the folks crowded around the food table to see. In the crotch of his jeans, Joe had a small rip near the zipper. As he shoveled the food into his mouth, one of his testicles slipped out of the hole in his pants.

Jenny Roberts was the first to notice. She pointed out Joe's "wardrobe malfunction" to Shey, who was tending bar.

"It was like an awful car wreck," Shey remembered. "You jus' couldn't look away."

Joe's exposed testicle was plump, slightly wrinkled, and completely bald. Many folks in the bar lost their appetites after that. It was the first and probably only time there was food left over after a Gene's Christmas Party. It is believed a picture of the testicle was taken. Word is, though, the picture was burned in the alley outside of the bar late one night in some unexplained cleansing ritual.

Joe Lucas's daughter was getting married. Joe was going to walk her down the aisle. His family had rented him a tuxedo at Daniel's men's store downtown. Al met him at Gene's. Joe had to go to Daniel's to get the tuxedo fitted.

Joe wasn't bathing much at the time. The salesperson at Daniel's would take a deep breath and hold it for several moments before going in to measure the more intimate areas of Joe's torso—under his arms, around his waist, and between his legs. When the tuxedo was ready, Al took Joe back to Daniel's to pick it up and went to

Gene's so Joe could try it on to see if it fit properly.

Joe sat in a booth at Gene's and took his shoes off. He was wearing a pair of white tube socks that stopped at his knees. In the process of pulling off his tight shoes, the ends of the socks were yanked away from his toes. As he walked to the men's room at Gene's to change into the tuxedo, it looked like he had two long white elephant trunks sticking out from each foot.

It is important to note that many of the men who frequented Gene's at this time had horrible aim when it came to directing their streams of piss into the toilet bowl. When Joe walked into the men's room in stocking feet, the floor was covered in urine. Joe put on the tuxedo as he stood in the urine. When he walked out of the bathroom, his socks were soaked, and the hemline of the tuxedo pants was wet.

The tuxedo fit perfectly. The many patrons at the crowded bar loudly cheered and whistled when Joe exited the bathroom. It looked as if he had just stepped out of a men's fashion magazine. Except as he walked through Gene's, the wet and heavy loose ends of each sock audibly slapped the bar room floor.

"Who keeps pissin' on the floor?" Al yelled.

"It's all your short dick motherfuckers you let in here, Al!" bar regular Dennis Moore barked.

"You better get that tuxedo off him quick, Al," Jim Bob said, "before it falls apart."

For decades, Joe helped Al at the bar. He did many things there, such as clean the bathrooms, sweep the floors, stock the coolers, take out the trash, and shovel the sidewalk. Al paid him a small daily wage as well as gave him free beer and hot dogs.

In more recent years, Joe mainly unclogged the toilets. The toilets would often get clogged as the paper towels in the bathrooms would inadvertently get tossed into them. Much thicker than toilet paper, the paper towels would get balled up in the drain and clog the toilet. Al had plungers and clothes hangers to push or pull the stuck paper towels out, respectively. He also had Joe, who if needed would reach into the toilet and pull the clog out with his hand. There were packages of rubber gloves under the sink in each bathroom for Joe to use.

One afternoon, Joe was eating potato chips and watching a detective show on the television in the back room like he often did. Lucy, who was bartending at the time, told Joe the men's room toilet needed to be unclogged. She set a pair of rubber gloves by the toilet for Joe to use. As she waited outside the bathroom, Joe walked in and had the toilet unclogged within minutes. Lucy peered into the bathroom and spotted the rubber gloves. They were still in the package--unopened. She looked to Joe who had returned to his seat in front of the television, back to snacking on the potato chips with his bare hands. She glanced back into the bathroom. The sink was dry. Not only were the rubber gloves unused, but it also seemed he didn't wash his hands after unclogging the toilet. Lucy looked back to Joe who licked his greasy and salty fingers, after shoveling more potato chips into his mouth.

"Oh, Jesus," she mumbled, before returning to the busy bar. "Please heaven, help us."

xxx

I'm goin' have sex tonight!

Eddie Doll was drunk out of his mind. He wobbled around on the front porch of Gene's, clutching the handrail so he wouldn't fall down. Al pulled up in his truck. Eddie asked Al if he could take him to Joyce's, a small dive bar downtown that served liquor. Al knew Eddie was too inebriated to go anywhere else. Eddie lived in an apartment a few blocks down the street from Gene's.

"No, Eddie," Al said, getting out of the truck. "You don't need to go downtown."

"Come on, Al, you sum-a-bitch. I have to go to Joyce's."

"Just stay here. I'll buy you a beer."

"I'm goin' have sex tonight!" Eddie cackled.

"No, you're not. Go back in the bar. I'll get you one more beer."

But Eddie was insistent as he continued to plead with Al to take him downtown to Joyce's.

"All right," Al finally said. "Get in the truck."

Unsteady on his feet and having trouble navigating the three-step porch of Gene's, Al helped Eddie into the passenger seat of the truck.

"All right, Eddie," Al said enthusiastically. "Let's go to Joyce's."

"I'm goin' have sex tonight!"

Al made one loop around the neighborhood and stopped in front of Eddie's apartment.

"Here you go, Eddie. Home. Safe and sound. Jus' like you wanted."

"Thanks, Al," Eddie said, struggling to get out of the truck before staggering into his apartment.

Eddie was back at Gene's early the next morning, not having any idea how he got home the day before but again wanting someone to give him a ride to Joyce's.

Eddie would often boast in Gene's about his many exploits after a few beers. Like his one-night stands with the ladies of Wheeling, West Virginia. "I got that Wheelin' feelin'," he would say.

Or his many girlfriends at Joyce's: "I'm goin' have sex tonight!"

Like his love for large-bodied women: "I like the kind of woman whose panties can fit around a wagon wheel."

Eddie used to brag about being a great hunter. He did bring jars of rabbit meat he had canned into Gene's one day. The meat in the jars still had fur on it. No one was quite sure where the rabbit came from. He claimed to have killed it.

"I shot a squirrel earlier," Eddie boasted one morning at Gene's.

"Bullshit! You've been drinkin' in here all morning."

"Well," Eddie said, reaching into a backpack he had placed on the barstool next to him. "Look at this, you sum-a-bitch."

He pulled from his bag a squirrel he assumed was dead.

"I killed this squirrel as the sun was comin' up."

Eddie slammed the bar with a stiff squirrel, who appeared to be dead. The squirrel turned out to be only stunned from Eddie's early morning shotgun blast. Suddenly, the wounded squirrel woke up and started bouncing on the bar like it was having a seizure. Before anyone could react, the startled squirrel hopped onto its feet and scampered across the bar, jumping over the many pint glasses of beer in front of it.

Frank Perilli was sitting at the end of the bar. As the squirrel approached him, he nonchalantly lifted his glass Coca-Cola bottle and smacked the squirrel on top of the head, knocking the poor creature unconscious.

Eddie was drinking at Gene's one morning. His girlfriend at the time was walking up Green Street towards the bar, looking for him. It seemed she knew Eddie had slept with another woman he'd met at Joyce's the night before. Al drove by Eddie's girlfriend on his way to Gene's.

"Hey, Eddie," Al called as he walked into the bar. "Someone's looking for you."

"Who?"

"Carla, and she's right outside."

"Shit! Don't tell her I'm here!" Eddie said in a panic as he dashed for the men's room.

The front door to Gene's banged open. Carla stomped into the bar. She probably weighed two hundred pounds more than Eddie, who was barely a hundred pounds at the time. Eddie was deathly afraid of her. He told everyone he only stayed with her because she had a lot of money.

"Where is he?" she growled.

"Who?" Al asked.

"You know who! That rat, Eddie Doll!"

"He's not here."

"He's always here! Where is he?"

"We haven't seen him," Al said, glancing at the few regulars sitting at the bar, who shook their heads.

Carla searched the back room and walked into the kitchen.

"I'll be back!" she snapped. "He's a dead man when I find him!"

After about fifteen minutes to make sure she wasn't coming back, Al went to the men's room. The door was locked. He could hear loud scuffling noises from inside.

"Eddie? Eddie?" he called through the door. "Open up, Eddie. She's gone."

The scuffling noises were louder.

"What the hell are you doing in there?" Al asked.

Eddie had hopped onto the toilet and attempted to climb out the window of the men's room. He was able to push the window screen out and had jimmied the window halfway open. He had one foot on the top of the toilet's tank and the other foot partially through the window above the toilet. He was stuck. And it was a good thing he was stuck. The men's room at the time was where the stage is now, and the window was probably twenty feet from the ground. If he would've managed to get out that window, he likely would have killed himself.

"Eddie, open up!" Al continued to call out.

"Come on! Unlock the door!"

"I can't! I'm stuck!"

It took Al and a few of the regulars most of the morning to unlock the bathroom door without breaking it. They eventually pulled Eddie from the window. They tried to carry him out of the bathroom, but he wouldn't let them. He was afraid Carla would come back. He ended up spending most of the afternoon hiding in there.

xxx

Jumpin' Purple Jesus

Left, Reed Davis. Right, bartender Brian Jones.

Former Gene's bartenders, Brian Jones and Charles Randolph, both got jobs bartending at a brand-new sports bar that had opened on High Street in Morgantown called The Sports Page.

This was big as there were no true sports bars in Morgantown in the 1990s. Most folks went to places like Gene's that had only one or two televisions to watch sports. The Sports Page opened, boasting nearly twenty televisions and a variety of video games as well as darts, billiards, foosball, and air hockey. It was quite popular with the college students. They also made a variety of overly sweet and highly potent specialty cocktails geared to the younger student crowd. One such drink was named Jumpin' Purple Jesus. It was a simple concoction of purple Kool-Aid and grain alcohol. Some of the regulars at Gene's loved it. They called it "that purple shit."

Brian and Charles would fill plastic pitchers full of it, and Al would drive to The Sports Page to pick them up. He would bring it back to Gene's, and he and several of the bar regulars would drink it in the basement of the bar. One night, the overly chatty Reed Davis had overindulged on the Jumpin' Purple Jesus.

"He got awful quiet," Al remembered. "He was sweating, and his face was white as a ghost. I knew I had to get him out of there before he got sick."

Reed was no taller than five feet, six inches, and weighed not much more than a hundred pounds.

"I lifted him up and hoisted him on my shoulder," Al said. "He was so drunk his body was like a wet noodle. I had my arms around his legs. His body fell over my shoulder, and the back of his head bounced off my back as I carried him upstairs. Before I know it, he starts puking, and the vomit is running down my back."

Reed, an out-of-work lawyer, was "taking care" of his 85-year-old mother. They lived together in her palatial, turn-of-the-century stone house on Grand Street, a few short blocks from Gene's. It should be noted that he spent much more time at Gene's than with his mother.

"I knew I had to get him home," Al went on. "I got him outside. I cleaned ourselves up and tossed his limp body into my truck. I drove him home and walked him to the porch. He gave me his house key as I had to unlock the front door for him. I opened the door. He staggered in sideways directly into an antique coffee table covered with assorted glass collectibles and knickknacks. He immediately fell onto the table, knocking the glass pieces to the floor. The crash of broken glass from the table overturning woke his mother. All the lights in the house instantly turned on."

"Is everything all right?" she called from the top of the stairs.

"Jus' bringing Reed home from the bar," Al called back.

"Thank you!"

The next morning Al pulled into South Park Exxon, the neighborhood gas station. Badly hungover, Reed was sitting in the passenger seat of his mother's car. He wore the hood of his sweatshirt over his head. The bill of a ball cap was pulled down over his eyes. He was pale and hunched over. His hands shook. Al tapped on his window. Reed pulled up his cap and opened the window.

"What's goin' on?" Al asked.

"Oh, you know, just taking care of mother."

Al glanced up as Reed's frail mother pumped gas into the car.

"Yeah, right." Al laughed.

xxx

Wednesday—Gene's special night

Current bartender Josh Graham regularly works Wednesday nights. He says if something crazy is going to happen at Gene's, it will be on a Wednesday.

Shirtless stranger searching for his phone.

It was a very cold and wintry Wednesday night. Gene's wasn't very busy. It was late. A few regulars sat around the bar. The front door

57

suddenly flew open. A heavy-set stranger no one had ever seen before stormed through. He wasn't wearing a shirt. His big belly hung over the front of his pants. He held an iPad that kept pinging. He appeared highly agitated, wildly scurrying about the bar like searching for a lover who was cheating on him.

"Can I help you?" Josh calmy asked as everyone in the bar stared at the crazed stranger.

"I lost my phone!"

"Your phone?"

"I was jus' dropped off here by an Uber. My iPad keeps pinging," said the shirtless stranger, walking behind each regular at the bar and studying the phone that sat by their pints of beer. "It says my phone's in here."

"Were you here earlier?" Josh asked, coming out from behind the bar.

"No."

"Then why do you think it's here?"

"Because my phone tracker says it is!" he growled, pointing to the screen of his iPad for Josh. "See!"

"I can help you look," Josh said.

The two of them spent nearly an hour searching every room of the bar from upstairs to downstairs. They searched under all the tables and booths. They scoured the kitchen and video poker room in back. They dug through all the trash cans. They searched in the pool room and speakeasy in the basement. His phone was not in Gene's.

"What's upstairs?" the man suddenly grumbled.

"Apartments."

The stranger hurried to the door.

"Wait! Wait!" Josh called as the wild interloper rushed outside.

Josh shook his head and the entertained regulars grinned as the heavy-footed stranger stomped up the stairs to the apartments above Gene's. He pounded on the doors of each apartment for several minutes, which seemed like an hour. No one at either apartment answered the door. Eventually, the stranger stomped back down to the bar.

"Why doesn't anyone answer their door?" the stranger asked after re-entering Gene's.

"Because you're shirtless, and it's two o'clock in the morning," Josh said.

Suddenly, a car pulled up. The angered stranger glanced outside.

"My Uber's here," he said. "I've got to go. I'll be back."

Those still at Gene's watched him get into the car and disappear into the night. No one has seen him since. And unfortunately, no one got the chance to ask why he wasn't wearing a shirt.

It was a Wednesday night. A hyperactive and wiry middle-aged man nobody remembered seeing before was in Gene's. He had a skullet haircut. He was completely bald on top with greasy, sandy blonde hair long in the back.

Anxiously bouncing off the walls, he seemingly was under the influence of more than just beer. He fidgeted in the front room, pacing behind the stools at the bar, before disappearing to the back, then outside, and quickly back inside through the front door. He continued this for many minutes as well as agitating several of the young woman in the bar at the time. Everyone at Gene's tried their best to avoid him.

Finally, he took a seat at the bar next to regular Kevin Davis. He tried to converse with Kevin, who either tried not to pay attention to him or pretended to be asleep—no one could tell. Not getting a response, the wired stranger stood from his stool, leaned forward, and lunged his body in front of Kevin's face. As he continued to try for a response, the long hair behind his head dangled for a few moments over the pint of beer in front of Kevin. It wasn't long until the end of his oily hair floated on the top of Kevin's beer.

"Back off, buddy!" called Josh Graham, who was bartending at the time. "Your hair is in his beer!"

"Fuck you!" the stranger barked back as bar regular Eli appeared from the back room.

Eli puffed out his chest and approached the bar. Along with Ted Kisko and Steven Seibert (who held his little dog, Yoko, during the entire episode), the three of them politely but sternly helped the crazed stranger out the front door and onto the sidewalk in front. No one has seen the stranger or his skullet since.

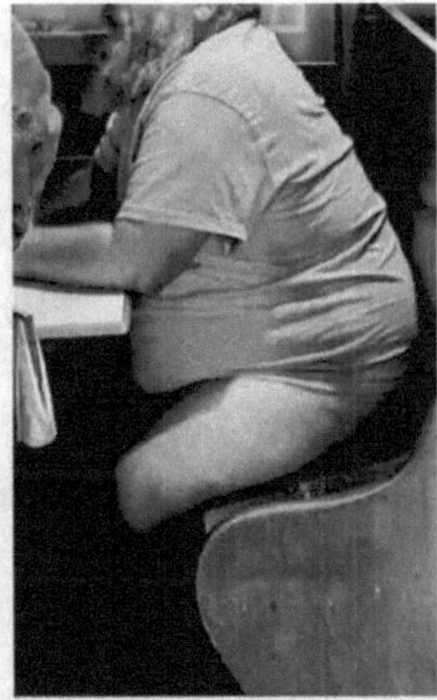

Nude stranger on each side of the booth.

On another Wednesday evening, an older man and woman came in the bar. No one at Gene's had ever seen them before either. The couple was sober and seemed nice. The man was overweight and wore a scruffy beard. He was quite filthy and didn't smell very good. His hands and fingernails were exceptionally dirty. They had a few beers and left sometime around 6 PM.

At a little after 10 PM, the couple had returned to Gene's. They were quite inebriated this time. Josh Graham was bartending. He got word they had been kicked out of the Met Pool Hall downtown. Because of their overly intoxicated state, he refused to serve beer to the couple. They asked if they could order some hot dogs to go. He agreed. So, they ordered fifteen chili dogs.

As Josh prepared their order, the couple took a

seat in one of the middle booths of the bar. At some point over the next several minutes, the man removed his shoes. His feet were dirty black. His toenails were yellow, curled, and appeared to be nearly two inches long. He had also removed his pants. His fat belly covered his small penis as his filthy bare ass soiled the wooden bench of the booth. Noticing the situation, Ted Kisko and Matt Smailes quickly formed a human wall in an attempt to block the view of the naked customer from others in the bar. At some point, the man moved from one side of the booth to the other, soiling that side as well. The naked and intoxicated man was eventually convinced to put his shoes and pants back on. He did it behind the human shield created by Kisko and Smailes, before attempting to leave the bar. The couple was so inebriated they needed help.

"He was so drunk," Josh remembered, "He didn't know where he was. He must've thought he was home in his living room and decided to get undressed."

The man and his lady friend left without taking their fifteen hot dogs. Josh passed them out to the folks at the bar. The soiled booth was blocked off with yellow police caution tape, preventing anyone from sitting there for the rest of the night. Shannon, the bartender the next morning, spent the first part of her shift disinfecting the entire booth with bleach.

The high cost of cheese

Al was walking into Gene's one morning. Don Burton and Dave Boken were walking out, both intoxicated. Their faces were flushed, and their gaits were unsteady. They giggled as they passed Al.

"Where in the hell are you two going?" Al asked.

"Helvetia," Don slurred.

"Helvetia?"

"To buy some cheese."

Helvetia is a small West Virginia town nestled in the mountains of Randolph County. It was settled by Swiss and German immigrants in 1869. The current population of Helvetia is thirty-eight people. It had been known around the state for decades because of the cheese made by the locals. Rogers McAvoy, a bar regular, had a house there many folks from Gene's would often visit during the many Helvetia festivals. But Helvetia is a two-hour drive from Morgantown. Don Burton was driving. He was nearly eighty years old—and drunk.

Burton and Boken were gone for a few hours when Al got a phone call from the magistrate's office in Clarksburg. On the way to Helvetia, Don Burton apparently had run an off-duty policeman and his family off Interstate 79 near the downtown Clarksburg exit. Burton had been arrested for driving under the influence.

Brian Jones, the bartender at Gene's at the time, was getting off his shift. He and Al drove to Clarksburg to bail Don Burton out. After the 45-minute drive, they parked in downtown Clarksburg. There was a steep set of steps that led up to the courthouse. Boken was napping on the top step with his head back, resting against one of the immense concrete columns at the entrance of the courthouse. Al kicked his foot.

"Where's Don?"

"Inside," Boken mumbled.

Al and Brian entered the courthouse and approached the bailiff at the receptionist's desk in the entrance.

"We're here for Don Burton," Brian said.

"Are you his son?" the bailiff asked.

"No, I'm his bartender."

Gene's II softball team.

Sadly, Don passed away on one of the softball fields at White Park while playing for the beer league level Gene's II softball team. The team wasn't any good. They used to joke that they led the league in "DUIs and not RBIs."

Nearly eighty years old, Don was one of their pitchers. He had a heart attack during a game and collapsed on the infield dirt behind the pitcher's mound. An ambulance was called, and he was strapped to a stretcher. Before leaving for the hospital, one of the paramedics emptied the contents of Don's pockets and gave them to a teammate. His pockets contained only three things: a joint, a bar napkin with a joke on it, and a condom.

xxx

This is not my vehicle

Dennis probably spent every night for the last ten years or so of his life at Gene's. He suffered from multiple sclerosis. He lived alone in an assisted living facility. He used two canes to walk. It often took him many minutes to get from his parked Chevy Blazer on the street in front to his stool at the end of the bar at Gene's. The regulars there were his family and his support group. He drank pony bottles of Budweiser and smoked cigars. He played the poker machines nightly. He was one of the first people in town to have an automatic starter installed in his Blazer. He would warm his truck before he was ready to leave the bar for the night. He almost always lingered in the Blazer as he would enjoy several hits of marijuana before coming into the bar and several after he left.

On one night as he played the poker machines in the back room of Gene's, someone yelled, "Dennis, your truck is on fire!"

"I'll be there in a minute," Dennis called back, seeming less concerned about the fire and more annoyed by the interruption as he was on a heated run of winning poker hands. "Jesus Christ," he mumbled.

As the Blazer filled with smoke, Al hurriedly pulled the driver's side door open. He was immediately engulfed in a thick plume of smoke that had the familiar skunk-like aroma of marijuana. Apparently, the lit end of the last joint Dennis smoked had fallen onto a towel on the floor mat of the truck. The towel had caught on fire, as well as the mat. As Al reached inside to pull the burning towel from the truck floor, he sensed someone behind him. Holding the smoldering towel and reeking of weed, he turned to a city policeman who held a lit flashlight in Al's face.

"I'm here to go on record," Al said without hesitation. "This is not my truck."

As Al tried to explain the situation to the cop, Peanut reached into the Blazer for the burning floormat. He grabbed the rubber part of the mat that had partially melted and was still quite hot, badly burning his hands. At the time, Brian Jones, a former Gene's bartender and current city fireman, arrived with a full fire crew in a ladder truck. He knew Dennis well from his Gene's bartending days. As his crew contained the small fire, Brian was able to convince the policeman the marijuana was part of Dennis's treatment for MS.

After the cop left, Dennis appeared outside. Although the inside badly smelled of weed and burnt rubber, he was assured his Blazer was safe to drive. Everyone was concerned about Peanut's burned hands. He had them wrapped in towels filled with ice. Dennis agreed to drive Peanut to the emergency room. Before they left, someone asked, "How are you going to get that awful burning smell out of your car?"

"Haven't you ever heard of Ozium, motherfucker?" Dennis replied.

Peanut ended up having third degree burns on each hand. Somehow, Dennis was able to use his health plan to cover the cost of Peanut's medical expenses.

I'll have a blue, blue, blue Christmas

"I walked into the bar," Al remembered. "The place had just opened. It was a Sunday. There were seven or eight people at the bar. Peanut hadn't shown up yet. I see Dave Snedeker, who didn't work for me, behind the bar. He's wearing a wizard outfit, long robe, tall pointy hat, you know. He's pouring beers and making hot dogs for everyone. He's filthy. His face is bright red, and his eyes are bloodshot and nearly closed. He reeked of alcohol and wood smoke. He'd been in Helvetia, camping all weekend at one of the festivals they have up there. I come to find out the only thing he's wearing is a pair of black Chuck Taylor high top sneakers. He's completely naked under the robe. I tell him, 'Dave, get out from back there. If the health department shows up, I'll lose my license and never get it back.'"

For more than a decade, the highlight of the Gene's Christmas party was when Dave Snedeker would climb onto the bar and sing the Elvis Presley song, "Blue Christmas." It was quite a scene, and everyone in the bar would excitedly sing along as Dave gyrated his lanky body to the popular Christmas carol. Even though Dave has long since moved away, numerous people ask every year if he will be back for the Christmas party to sing the song.

XXX

You may have heard of me — Juan Barnez

Al used to have a video surveillance camera in his office in the basement of Gene's. Sometimes he'd disappear downstairs and watch the activity at the bar on the camera from the basement. One time when Al was in the basement, one of the regulars, John Barnes, moved from a barstool to behind the bar. The bartender had disappeared to the kitchen to put away the food for the night. He was taking an exceptionally long time, and John wanted one last beer. He took a bottle of beer from the cooler, intending to pay for it when the bartender returned.

There was a pay phone on the wall where the potato chip rack is now. During that time before mobile phones became prevalent, people at the bar would use the pay phone to call out of the place. Calls would also come in on that phone for people who were at the bar. The number on the pay phone was the listing for Gene's in the phonebook.

After Barnes took the beer and returned to his seat, Al called the pay phone from his office in the basement as a joke. Someone near the phone answered it. In a disguised voice, Al asked for Barnes.

"Barnes, it's for you."

Looking somewhat surprised as no one called

him at the bar, he walked over to the phone.

"Hello."

"John," Al said in a spooky, Wizard of Oz-like voice. "This is your conscience. Put the beer back."

With a confused expression, Barnes hung up the phone, grabbed his coat, and quickly left the bar, leaving the beer behind. No one saw him for weeks after that.

xxx

In need of a good waxing

"The Wiz [Randy Neiman] and a couple of the young guys I had working the door for me on

70

busy nights, Aaron and Booter Ryan, did this thing they called *waxing*. They would whack each other in the forehead with a forceful open-handed slap when the other wasn't expecting it. Sometimes it looked like they really would hurt each other. One night around closing, I was washing glasses behind the bar with my head down. The Wiz is on the barstool across from me. I looked up at him from behind the sink, and without warning, he violently smacked me in the middle of my forehead. He hit me so hard that I stumbled back, nearly knocking me out. I saw stars. It took me a couple minutes to regain my composure as he laughed and laughed.

"I didn't say anything. I finished washing the glasses and slowly dried my hands with a towel. Without any warning as he continued to laugh, I whacked him with my open hand with so much force I knocked him clear off his stool. He hit the floor with a loud thud. I leaned over the bar and looked at him. He didn't move. I thought I had killed him. I moved from behind the bar to check on him. After a moment or so, he started to blink his eyes and shake his head. Then he glared at me with a big smile.

"Good one, Al!" he said with a laugh. "You got me! You got me good!"

The Wiz had started dating a woman who had recently moved into the Greenmont neighborhood. She was an attractive middle-aged woman—a former beauty queen. He seemed to be quite enamored with her. For the first several weeks they were together, he was rather tight-lipped about the relationship. He would drink several beers at Gene's each night and suddenly disappear down the street for a few hours. He'd always return to Gene's for a nightcap before heading home. On one night, he wasn't his normally boisterous self on his return to the bar. He looked lost and a little distracted, like he was trying to hide something. He never would say much about what happened during those hours he would be gone, and no one asked. Finally, someone did.

"How's the new girlfriend?"

"She's got a tail," he answered without hesitation.

"What?"

"She's got a tail."

"A tail? On her body?"

"Yeah, a tail."

"Where?"

"Bottom of her back."

"A real tail?"

"Yeah, a real tail. It freaked me out at first."

"And now?"

"It kinda turns me on," he quietly confessed, like telling a secret.

"Turns you on?"

"It moves when we get intimate."

"Moves?"

"And the more excited we get, the faster it moves."

"And you've touched it."
"Of course I've touched it."
"What's it feel like?"
"A tail. It feels like a tail."

xxx

"Paranoia is just a higher state of awareness." —
Tom Dunham

It was well after two in the morning. Al was closing the bar. He got a phone call. It was the Sheriff's office. They had just arrested Tom Dunham, one of the regulars at the bar, for driving under the influence. He needed to be bailed out. Al told the Sheriff he'd be down in a few minutes.

When he got to the Sheriff's office, he discovered Tom was not locked up in a jail cell. He was sitting behind a desk in the back office in the Sheriff's seat. His feet were up on the Sheriff's desk. Everyone in the office was laughing. Overly inebriated, Tom had been entertaining the night staff with jokes and stories as he waited for Al to bail him out. When Al finally arrived, a cheer rang out.

"What took you so long?" Tom asked.

"Why'd you call me?"

"You were only person I could think of who was still awake and had $400 in cash on them at this hour."

xxx

"The only ones getting any ass around here are rock stars, drug dealers, and *bar owners!*"

—Tom Dunham

Spiders from Greenmont

Roadie made a large snowball one evening after a heavy January snowstorm. He had the bartender put the snowball in the freezer where the frosty pint glasses were stored. One afternoon many months later, on a hot August day, Reed Davis was running his mouth and joking it up, not only annoying Roadie but others at the bar.

Roadie asked the bartender for the snowball. It had become a softball-sized ball of ice at that point. With Reed's head turned, Roadie called to him. Reed turned and Roadie threw the ice ball directly at Reed's head. It violently exploded on Reed's forehead, dropping him from his barstool and knocking him unconscious. After many minutes, Reed finally woke up. He had a fist-sized knot on his forehead that was bleeding. He looked at Roadie.

"Jesus, Roadie! What was that for?"

"I'm not in the mood to hear that whiney little mouth of yours."

Roadie had an overly enormous, bubble-shaped, and malformed right bicep. The malformation was likely caused by a tear in his bicep muscle that had never been repaired. Charles, the bartender at the time, jokingly told everyone that the large bulge in Roadie's upper arm was filled with spiders. One night at closing after a long shift of beer-drinking, Roadie stumbled on the uneven sidewalk out in front of the bar on his way to the parking lot. He badly injured his ankle.

Thinking it might be broken, a couple of the regulars at the bar drove him to the emergency room to get an X-ray. The emergency room doctor walked into the examination room and nearly fell over, grabbing his chest. It looked as if he'd just seen a ghost.

"What happened to your arm?" he asked Roadie, gently touching the bicep with a pair of forceps.

"It's my ankle, motherfucker, not my arm!"

xxx

Vacation is all I ever wanted

Top left, Is Spuds safe? Bottom left, Chris A and Spuds. Right, Spuds returns.

Spuds MacKenzie was a fictional dog character used by Budweiser in promotional ads in the 1980s. A plastic replica of the Spuds McKenzie dog, generously donated by Leah Adkins, has resided on the top of one of the beer coolers in Gene's for many years. It is still there today. Sometime during a summer years ago, Spuds mysteriously went missing. When no one was watching and during the time the bar's surveillance cameras were non-functional, a regular of the bar had pulled Spuds from the top of the cooler and disappeared into the night.

Photos of Spuds began to appear in the mail at Gene's, showing the plastic dog at different locales in the country. There was a photo of Spuds on a boat in Deep Creek, Maryland. He was photographed on the beach in the Outer Banks of North Carolina. There was a picture of Spuds in the parking lot of Busch Stadium before a baseball game in St. Louis. There were racy photos of Spuds in random motel room beds in compromised positions with different half-dressed young ladies.

Even to this day, the identity of Spuds's kidnapper has never been revealed. During Spuds's disappearance, a few folks who regularly hung out at the bar were falsely accused. One of whom was Chris A., who had nothing to do with the kidnapping of the plastic dog mascot.

On one winter night without fanfare or announcement, Spuds, hidden in an unmarked brown paper bag, was secretly dropped off under a pinball machine in the back room of Gene's. The Spuds replica had been gone for nearly five months. It wasn't discovered until early one morning when Joe Lucas found it as he mopped the floor in the back room. There was a great celebration that day as Gene's beloved Spuds MacKenzie had been returned. The raucous bar patrons drank late that night, draining one keg of Budweiser and two kegs of Bud Light.

Still curious about the identity of Spuds's kidnapper, many of the regulars at the bar constantly harassed Chris A. They were sure he was the villain. He vowed to get back at them. He planned to take Spuds himself, and he would secretly attempt to do it right in front of their faces when the bar was the busiest. He planned to take Spuds during the annual Gene's Christmas party.

But he didn't account for two very important details about his plan. One, the beer was free all night during the Christmas party. He had been at the party for hours and was quite intoxicated when it was time to pull off the heist. And two, the top of the beer cooler where Spuds was perched was higher than he expected. He would have to hoist himself off something to reach the plastic dog.

He decided he would use the front of the hot dog-steaming station. It was positioned next to the beer cooler he needed to scale. The station consisted of a bun steamer and a series of stainless-steel pots that contained hot dogs in boiling water and pots of simmering chili sauce and warmed barbecue. The water that steamed the buns, cooked the hot dogs and warmed the chili, and barbecue was heated by a flame that came from a natural gas line underneath. There also was a wooden cutting board connected to the front of the cooking station where the hot dogs and other foods were prepared.

Chris waited until the end of night as the party was winding down to make his move. After the bartender left with the steel pot of chili sauce to put away in the kitchen in back, Chris made a sudden dash for Spuds. He leaped towards the hot dog station, positioning his right foot on the cutting board in front. He didn't realize there was no support underneath it, and the entire station flipped forward, violently slamming Chris backwards onto the floor behind the bar, nearly knocking him unconscious.

Suddenly dazed and stuck like an upside-down turtle on its shell, unable to turn over, Chris tried lift his drunken body off the floor as hot water from the hot dog steaming station puddled around him.

"I was downstairs changing a keg in the basement," Al recalled. "I heard what sounded like an explosion, then a loud thump on the floor above me. All of a sudden, water is pouring through the ceiling into the basement. His fall had disconnected the gas line. He could've blown up the place!"

Before Chris could flee the scene, Dennis Moore, the man in the late stages of MS, from his seat in the chair behind the bar, pinned Chris with the ends of his two canes. He leaned over Chris with the ends of the canes stabbed against each side of Chris's chest into his shirt.

"I don't know what you're tryin' to pull, motherfucker," Dennis barked over him, "but you ain't goin' nowhere!"

Chris was banned from Gene's for a short time after that. And since then, no one has attempted to kidnap Spuds MacKenzie again.

xxx

The first rule of Mug Club is do not talk about Mug Club

"Welcome to the Al Bonner School of Business." Al laughed. "I thought the Mug Club was a great idea, you know. It would maybe bring new

80

people into the bar as well as be a nice gesture to my regulars who came in there all the time. I still have a lot of those mugs somewhere in storage."

The Mug Club was an experiment that lasted only two years. The idea was simple. A person would buy a personalized ceramic mug for $25. All the mugs were stored on a special wooden rack behind the bar. Whenever a person would buy a beer with their mug, their second beer would be free. They were allowed one free beer a day.

"Boy, what a mistake," Al went on. "I lost my ass. We were open from early in the morning until two at night. We had multiple bartenders in and out of there all day. The regulars knew when their shifts changed. They'd come in several times a day, getting free mugs of beer. They were only supposed to get one a day. We had trouble keeping track of 'em. I think there were competitions going on to see who could get the most free mug beers in a day."

It's also important to note that on the anniversary of the day the mug was purchased, the mug owner got to drink free beer all day long.

"And I had two large groups who bought mugs on the same day," Al shook his head. "There were the Groundhogs. A group of about six or so of my older regulars who had bought their mugs on February 2, Groundhog Day. And there were the Christmas Carolers. A younger group of regulars who got their mugs on December 20. There may have been eight of them."

"So, you can imagine what happened on December 20 and February 2," Al continued. "It was total mess. And all day to those two groups meant *all day*! They would be waiting at the front door for me to open. And they wouldn't leave until last call. The caroler group would be singing along to Christmas carols on the jukebox all day. They ran off business with all the drunken singing. They took over the front room. They played electric football on the long table. They would drink nearly two kegs of free beer themselves."

"And the Groundhogs were worse!" Al laughed out loud. "They would bring in bottles of whiskey. The whiskey didn't make them any drunker. The beer made them drunk enough. The whiskey just kept them going all day. I had to cut them off after two free kegs. And it was still daylight! Then, I had to give 'em all rides home."

"Do you ever think about bringing the Mug Club back?" someone listening from the bar asked.

"No," Al answered without hesitation.

Mug Club also is not to be confused with the Jug Club. The Jug Club was a popular group of young ladies who were regulars and bartenders at Gene's in the 1990s. The Jug Club included Laurel, Kris, Stacey, and Ronna. According to everyone you ask, the bar was always a lot more fun when they were there.

A big tipper

Charles was living in an apartment above Gene's at the time. He also was working as a bartender there. On days off, he often would go barhopping through town and cab it back to his apartment at the end of a night.

One evening a cab pulled up in front of Gene's. The bar wasn't too busy. The regulars watched Charles get out and stagger to the door outside that led to his apartment upstairs. After a few minutes, the cab driver entered Gene's. His cab idled in the street in front of the bar.

"Does anyone know the guy who I just dropped off?"

"Yeah," Mike Moran, the bartender, said. "That's Charles. He lives upstairs and works here."

"He left me this for the fare," the cabbie said, holding up a check written for one million dollars.

"How much was the fare?" Moran asked.

"Six bucks."

"Here's a twenty," Moran said, pulling the bill from his tip jar. "Keep the change."

"Thanks!" The cab driver nodded.

He turned to leave but stopped.

"What should I do with this?" he asked Moran, holding up the million-dollar check.

"I'd keep it. Maybe try to cash it. It could be good. You never know with Charles."

After moving away from Morgantown, former bartender and regular, Charles Randolph was at Gene's during a visit. Dave Davis came into the bar and spotted Charles.

"Hey Charles, what are you doing here?"

"Jus' passin' through," he answered.

"How long are in town for?"

"Until I sober up." Charles paused. "Which could be years."

xxx

Steve Brady versus the barflies and cockroaches

During a bartender shift change on a Wednesday evening, Josh Graham came in to replace Steve Brady. Steve was trying to close out his register and update Josh on some bar-related business before he ended his shift. There was a guy sitting across from them at the bar. He always came in when Steve worked. He liked to talk to Steve about God, religion, and other like topics. He kept interrupting Steve and Josh, greatly delaying the shift change and Steve's ability to get out of the bar after a long shift.

Eventually, Steve ignored him. Because of this, the guy turned his attention to Josh who tried to be polite and listen to what he had to say. The guy reached for his phone and played a contemporary gospel song for Josh. As Steve tried to talk to Josh during the shift closeout, the guy at the bar turned up the volume on his phone to an excessively loud level.

"Here, listen to this," he called out to Josh over the noise of the song. "You'll like this one."

Unable to talk with Josh, Steve angrily turned to the guy.

"Ronnie! Take your fucking revival to the back room or get the hell out of the bar! We're busy here!"

It was St. Patrick's Day 2020, and the Governor's office was about to shut down all businesses in West Virginia because of *Covid*. That would be the last night for many months that bars, restaurants, schools, universities, and most public places would be open. Everyone knew that. Gene's was packed. Steve Brady was bartending. It was getting late. One of the regulars, Ryan Jeffers, was somewhat intoxicated but still going strong, knocking back numerous tall boy cans of Pabst Blue Ribbon beer.

"Steve," I said, leaving the crowded bar at one o'clock in the morning, "It'll just be you, Ryan, and the cockroaches when you lock this place up."

Ryan was indeed the last person to leave the bar. He had trouble standing as he bounced from one wall to the next after backing off his barstool. Steve knew he couldn't let Jeffers drive home. Both Casey Williams and Jeff Antonini refused to

let Ryan stay at their places. So, Steve called him
an Uber. Steve used his own account because
Ryan didn't have one.

When Steve woke up the next day, he checked
his Uber account. It was billed $250—a cleaning
fee. Apparently, Ryan had vomited in the Uber on
his way home.

"The guy drove like a maniac," Ryan would
later say.

He blamed the barfing mishap on the winding
and hilly Point Marion Road and not the gallon
and half of cheap beer he guzzled that evening on
an empty stomach. That was the last night Gene's
would be open for almost a year.

xxx

The ballad of Little Chicken

Ed Biser, a long-time Gene's regular and Vietnam
vet, called himself Little Chicken. Despite his
small physical size, he could be quite scary to
someone who didn't know him. He chain-
smoked cigarettes and spoke with a throaty rasp.
He was feisty and more than a little crazy. And he
drank a lot.

It was a Thursday sometime in the 1990s.
Gene's was packed—standing room only. Al
used to charge fifty cents for a draft of beer on
Thursday nights. The place would fill with
college students looking for cheap beers before

heading downtown to the more student-friendly bars. Gene's would get so busy on those nights Al would open a small serving area with a keg in the basement to accommodate all the people. He needed a door man outside and several bartenders. Little Chicken got there late and was stuck by the front door of Gene's. He was making wisecracks to everyone who walked in.

Andy "Skinny" Miller, a regular patron of Gene's, entered.

"What's the password?" Little Chicken jokingly asked.

"Password?" Skinny asked, not knowing Little Chicken was joking.

"What's the password?" Little Chicken asked again. "You can't come in without the password."

"I don't know the password."

Without warning, Little Chicken grabbed Skinny by the testicles.

"Now, tell me the password!"

Skinny's face turned red and his eyes widened as Little Chicken tightened his grip on Skinny's nuts.

"The password, asshole. I'm not letting go until you tell me the password."

"But I don't know the password," Skinny squealed as he bent his body forward in obvious pain as Little Chicken continued to squeeze his testicles.

"Let go of him, Little Chicken," Mike Roh spoke up. He stood nearly a foot taller than Little

Chicken. "There is no password."

Little Chicken referred to Mike as Big Bird.

"You jus' ruined the joke, Big Bird," Little Chicken said in disappointment as he released Skinny's balls from his grasp.

For a time, Little Chicken didn't have a driver's license. He had a collapsible bike he would ride to Gene's. It supposedly was very expensive. It was the first time anyone at Gene's had seen such a bike. When he was too drunk to ride home, he oftentimes would get a ride home. He would take his bike with him as it would fold in half and fit into most vehicles.

On one occasion when he was quite intoxicated, there was no one at Gene's to give him a ride home. Al had to stay and work at the bar.

"You need to push that thing home tonight," Al warned him. "You're too drunk to ride it."

Not listening, Little Chicken attempted to climb onto the bike and ride it home. He wrecked twice before getting more than a block away from Gene's. Al and few others watched from the sidewalk in front. They couldn't help but laugh as Little Chicken comically tried to climb onto the collapsible bike for a third time. The impact of the wrecks had folded the bike together. At this point, Little Chicken couldn't figure out the front of the bike from the back. The two wheels were pointing in different directions.

Carl, another Vietnam vet and regular of the bar, appeared from down the street and approached Little Chicken, who had fallen again, attempting to help him. Carl was just as drunk as Little Chicken.

"You know," Carl scolded Al and the others, "some things that appear funny are not."

After several minutes, Carl finally gathered Little Chicken and the bike.

"Come on, soldier," he said. "I'm taking you home."

Holding his hand, Carl dragged Little Chicken and the folded bike down Green Street for a few blocks. However, Little Chicken lived several streets further away from Gene's than Carl did. Once they got to Carl's house, he left Little Chicken on his own to go the rest of the way. Somehow in his inebriated state, Little Chicken got his bike snapped back together and climbed on top. He made it two blocks before wrecking on Brockway Avenue. A pedestrian witnessed the wreck and called 9-1-1.

Al could hear the sirens at Gene's. He worried they had something to do with Little Chicken. He got one of the regulars to watch the bar. He drove towards the sound of the sirens. He could see blue and red lights flashing in the distance. On Brockway, there were police cars, an ambulance, and a fire truck. He could see Little Chicken. His limp body was spread-eagled in the middle of the road. His head was bleeding. Paramedics were fitting a brace around his neck. Al got out of his truck and approached a policeman.

"How's is he?" Al asked. "I know him."

"He should be okay," he said. "Likely has a concussion. They're taking him to the hospital for tests to make sure."

Al got in his truck and drove to Little Chicken's house. Al knocked on the door. Little Chicken's brother answered.

"Your brother wrecked his bike. They're putting him in an ambulance and taking him to the hospital. He was bleeding from the head."

"He'll be fine," his brother said. "Is the bike all right?"

Al shrugged as Little Chicken's brother closed the door.

As it turned out, Little Chicken would be okay, but the bike would not. Unfortunately, it had been mangled.

xxx

Werewolves, ghosts, and Elvira

"It must be a full moon tonight," Lucy and the other bartenders would often say during wild nights at Gene's.

A full moon was known to bring out the craziest of Morgantown. There have been two werewolves at Gene's (at least, they thought they were werewolves). One lived upstairs. The other bartended for a short time.

Grady is a longtime regular and a longtime resident of one of the apartments above the bar at Gene's. He can often be seen and heard howling at full moons over Wilson Avenue. From his apartment, he would often play the internet jukebox in Gene's from the app on his phone to entertain (or mostly annoy) the customers in the bar below his apartment. His song of choice was "Tiptoe Through the Tulips," by Tiny Tim.

The other so-called werewolf was former Gene's bartender, John Marcus. During a heat wave in the summer of 1991, he really believed he was a werewolf. He had friends lock him in the trunks of their cars on nights of full moons. As he would explain, this was to protect the citizens of Morgantown after he supposedly transitioned from a man to a werewolf on those nights. He wouldn't come out of the trunk until early the next day, claiming the werewolf phase had ended and he had turned back to a human.

On one occasion during a full moon, a group of Gene's regulars watched from the front window as a partially dressed, hunched-over man crazily dashed up and down Wilson Avenue. Several of them went outside to get a closer look at the shadowy figure. The man wore no shoes or shirt, only a pair of shredded dress pants. Upon closer inspection, someone identified the stranger as John Marcus. After several mad passes by Gene's, Marcus, badly out of breath, finally entered the bar, growling and barking.

Sometime earlier that evening, Marcus had covered his body with corn syrup and stuck handfuls of human hair he had collected from the floors of different barber shops onto his back, arms, chest, legs, hands, feet, and face. The folks at the bar were both amused and somewhat horrified by what stood before them.

But not as horrified as John's girlfriend when he was dropped off at her house in the middle of the night, still covered in sticky blobs of the human hair that had belonged to complete strangers.

There have been numerous claims of Gene's being haunted. On a busy night soon after Al had purchased the bar, he swore he saw Gene, the original owner.

"The bar was busy," Al recalled. "I was taking it all in. Happy about my decision to buy the place, you know. The front door slowly opened. I swore I saw Gene who had been dead for nearly a decade stick his head in the bar. He looked at me and smiled—like he was happy for me. Suddenly, he was gone. Not believing what I saw, I hurried to the front door. I looked outside, but no one was there. I asked the guys standing at the bar if anyone had come in. No one saw anyone enter. And I hadn't been drinking at all that night."

The view of Gene's front door from back of bar.
Photo by Ted Kisko.

"On another night," Al continued. "I had just closed. I was putting away the food and cleaning up the dishes. As I walked by the stairs that led to the basement, a glowing light caught my attention. I glanced down the steps to the glow. I swear I saw Gene standing at the bottom of the stairs. It still freaks me out."

"And another time more recently," Al went on. "A college kid pointed to a picture of Gene on the wall and asked me who that was. I told him it was Gene, the original owner. He asked me if he was still alive. I laughed and said that he died in 1979. The kid said he'd just seen him standing in the pool room alone by himself. After all these years, I guess, it seems, Gene is still here, looking over the place."

After a full afternoon of beers at Gene's, Roadie would torment some of the regulars as well as Al by flinging beer coasters at them like frisbees. It drove Al crazy, and Roadie knew it. He was constantly warned to stop through the years but never did.

Roadie also especially loved the song "Elvira," by the Oak Ridge Boys. Oftentimes after he was drunk, he enjoyed singing along to the chorus when the song played on the jukebox:

"My heart's on fire on fire for Elvira
Giddy up, oom poppa, oom poppa, m-ow, m-ow
Giddy up, oom poppa, oom poppa, m-ow, m-ow
Heigh-ho silver away!"

Years after Roadie had died, multiple people have claimed to have seen him in the basement and back room of Gene's at different times. Al swears that flying coasters would often zip by him and Lucy late at night when they were the only ones in the bar. The old CD-style jukebox at Gene's would occasionally play a random song when it hadn't been played for a while. On the first anniversary of Roadie's death when the bar was about to close, the song "Elvira" suddenly started to play.

"The bar immediately got cold. I got goosebumps," Al said. "Nobody had played the jukebox all day. It felt like he was standing there with us."

Does anyone own a cement mixer?

A longtime Gene's regular had been overserved. Al wanted to give him a ride home. Even though the guy lived only a few blocks away from Gene's, he was in no condition to drive or even walk. He adamantly refused the ride from Al. The man lived at home with his elderly father. He didn't want his father to see him needing assistance to get home. He was a middle-aged man at the time. But Al persisted, dragging the regular from a booth in Gene's, through the front door, down the sidewalk, and into his truck. The two of them aggressively grappled with each other the whole way. Al finally locked him in the truck and sped off to the man's house. Once parked in the driveway, Al glared at him.

"You need to go inside," he said.

The regular glanced at his house. His dad watched from the front window.

"You did it now, Al," he said.

"Did what?"

"My dad's dead," he solemnly answered, thinking he had greatly disappointed his father.

"You killed him."

"What are you talk—"

The man reared his right arm back and forcefully punched Al in the side of the face. Now exceptionally angry, Al threw open his door and rushed to the passenger side of truck. He ripped the door open and pulled the man from the truck. He had been wearing a Sony Walkman tape player, which hit the ground. Its batteries rolled the down the driveway and into the street.

Al sped back to Gene's. Before entering, he stood on the sidewalk in the front and stared at the building. A couple of regulars were standing on the steps of the entrance and studied Al.

"What are you looking at?" one of them asked.

"If I hit the lottery, I'm goin' cut a large hole in the top of this building and fill it with cement." Al said, before chuckling. "But I know guys like Joe Lucas, Boken, and Roadie will be here early in the morning with chisels and hammers, trying to bust their way in."

Chapter 6
Music, Art, And Community

Behind the microphone from the Gene's stage. Photo by Ted Kisko.

Live music didn't come to Gene's until the late 1990s. Singer-songwriter Owen Davis, a bar regular and long-time friend of Al, asked if his band could play a show at Gene's in support of the new record he was releasing. Al set them up in the back room among the pinball machines and video games. The space was tight, and there were limited places to stand and watch the show. During the performance, multiple people, including former bartender Casey Bicanich, climbed onto the pinball machines for a better view of the band. As he sat there and watched, Casey broke through the thick glass on top of one of the pinball machines. Al knew he had to make some changes in the bar if he wanted to have music shows regularly.

Owen Davis and the Free Hummus All Stars in the back room before the stage. Photo by Jenny Roberts.

That incident led to Al building a stage in the main bar in the early 2000s with the help of bar regular and friend, Mike Roh. The two of them removed truckloads of old wood siding from a dilapidated farmhouse where Al's mother had grown up just outside of Morgantown. They also found three 16-foot wood beams that would be used to frame the stage. One of the beams was filled with termites. After multiple heavy treatments with insecticide, the beam was brought inside Gene's. Friend, regular, and legendary Gene's dart thrower Corky Kershner helped them frame the stage.

"You two are the only guys I know who brought termites inside of a building," he joked.

On the back wall of the stage, Mike later added a large wooden sculpture shaped like the state of West Virginia. It still hangs there over two decades later. Local musician Kim Monday generously donated all the necessary sound equipment as well as a lighting system for the stage. The stage is affectionally called the Owen Davis Stage.

Painting by Malissa Baker of Owen Davis and the Free Hummus All Stars.

Gene's is known for not having a cover charge at the door for shows. The money collected for the bands and performers comes from tips from the crowd and generous donations by Al at the end of the night.

"Some bands make more money on a night than I do," Al joked.

There has only been one ticketed show. That was for Bill Kirchen, the Titan of the Telecaster and former lead guitarist of Commander Cody and His Lost Planet Airmen. Since the stage was built, hundreds of local and touring national musical acts have performed at Gene's. Touring acts have included Lydia Loveless, Clem Snide, Langhorne Slim, The Dusty 45's, Rose's Pawn Shop, The Americans, Jaded Ravins, Abe Partridge, among hundreds of others.

Renowned music stars on tour with the infamous Gene's hat. Left, Tyler Childers. Middle, Charles Wesley Godwin. Right, John R. Miller. All played at Gene's early in their careers.

Touring acts. Left top, The Living Deads. Left bottom, The Americans. Center, The Dusty 45's. Right top, Bill Kirchen. Right bottom, Rose's Pawn Shop.

Recent performances by touring acts Jaded Ravins, Abe Partridge, and Charles Wesley Godwin.

Crack house

Patrons on a barstool at Gene's often exposed their butt cracks (aka, *plumber's crack*). And there has always been a short curtain that ran along the lower half of the front window of the bar. Little did Al know, but this curtain hid some of the butt cracks from the outside world. The curtain was once removed for cleaning. Roadie, who often sat at that end of the bar, was (and still is) the butt crack champion of the world. With no curtain to block the view, the neighborhood kids would line Wilson Avenue in front of the bar after school. They would gawk, point, and laugh at the long deep crevice that jutted up from the back of Roadie's ill-fitting blue jeans. The situation got so bad that one of the parents complained to Al. A new curtain was quickly returned to the window (the old one fell apart during washing) and has never been removed since.

Owen Davis cover of his record Crack House.

Local musician and bar regular Owen Davis wrote several songs inspired by Gene's. Some of them were included on his 1994 record *Crack House*. Owen is always quick to point out that the word *crack* in his record's title doesn't refer to the illegal street drug but the butt cracks constantly being flashed at Gene's.

Owen hired a professional photographer, John Bright, then with a local newspaper and now owner of the popular Purple Fiddle music club and B&B in Thomas, West Virginia, to take a photo for the cover of the record. The idea was to secretly snap a non-staged shot of an exposed butt crack at the bar. Soon after John arrived, there were multiple opportunities for the perfect photo. However, Tom Dunham was watching and figured out what was happening.

"I see what's going on here," Tom called out. "This is a clear case of exploitation, takin' advantage of these fine, hard-workin' fellows here."

Every time John would try to take a picture, Tom would put his hand in front of the exposed butt crack of the unsuspecting Gene's patron, blocking the chance for a photo.

Because of Tom's objection, the plan was changed. The butt crack photo for the record cover would be staged. It was amazing how many of the regulars wanted their butt cracks to be used. In the end, the butt cracks in the photo chosen for the cover belonged to John Barnes and his cousin.

An amazing letter to Owen from a fan from Los Angeles:

"... Dear Owen,

I've never met you and I hope you don't mind fan letters! I'm a professional musician living in Los Angeles. Finding you on Facebook gives me the opportunity to share with you a story that directly involves your music. You have no idea...

At some point in the mid '90s (I was a kid), my uncle spotted your "Crack House" album at a music store. Because of the amusing front cover photo, he bought a copy and gave it to me, knowing I would appreciate the humor in it. Upon receiving it, I chuckled and then set the CD aside for the time being.

January 31, 1997: I am 14 years old, growing up in a small town in Maine. My best friend Ed was at my house for a jam session and a sleep over that night. After my parents had gone to bed, Ed and I (for the first but not the last time) snuck into my parents' liquor cabinet and grabbed a bottle of vodka and some orange juice from the fridge. This was the night I first became a mischievous, rebellious teenager. I had never been drunk before and I believe Ed had only been drunk once. We mixed screwdrivers in my bedroom and while getting inebriated, listened to "Crack House". I'll never forget the fun of feeling drunk for the first time, and may I add, with your music as the soundtrack. From then on, whenever Ed came to my house to stay over, the ritual was get drunk (and later on, a little weed smoking too) while listening to "Crack House." For me, the sound of your singing voice and the songs on that album have always been synonymous with the taste of screwdrivers and the memories of surreptitiously boozing with my buddy in that room in the middle of the night. Special times indeed!

Fast forward to 2012. I'd been living in California and Ed was married, living in North Carolina. Still best friends and now "responsible adults". We both traveled to Maine in June for my wedding. A few days before I got hitched, Ed and I took a road trip while listening to your other five albums that I'd recently purchased through CD Baby. (We especially got a laugh out of "Columbia House Wants Me Back".)

Since then, I've spent considerable time listening to all six CDs. I appreciate the lyrical humor and clever writing, as well as the sonic quality and fine musicianship. I'm a big fan!! Now I see on FB you have a new CD. I will purchase it!

I hope this letter didn't bore you or seem kitschy. As silly as the story may be, I felt the need to tell you that your music has, for many years, held an amusing presence in the lives of two goofballs from Maine.

Sincerely,
Seth Romano . . ."

Everyone's favorite townie bar

Al had just started booking music regularly at Gene's. Aaron Hawley's band 85 Flood was scheduled to play a Saturday night show for the first time at Gene's with another legendary local band, The Emergency. Aaron was thrilled to have the opportunity to play there as he still often refers to Gene's as "the greatest bar on the planet."

He and his eager bandmates awkwardly lugged their guitars and amplifiers in through the front door of the bar. Peanut was working. He quietly watched as the members of the two bands stacked their equipment inside of Gene's. Aaron approached Peanut looking for instructions about the set-up for the show.

"We're the band playing here tonight," he excitedly announced to Peanut.

Peanut didn't initially respond. He blankly stared at Aaron for a moment.

"So," he finally said, before walking away to wait on another customer.

A Very Townie Christmas. Left corner, 85 Flood with William Matheny. Right corner, even Al joined in on the fun.

For many years, 85 Flood would play a show on the Friday before Christmas with other local bands, such as Haley Slagle and the Hardway, William Matheny and the Frustrations, and The Border States, J. Marinelli, Diablo Sandwich, among others. The event was dubbed A Very Townie Christmas. It always drew large crowds to Gene's. It was a night for those who had moved away and had returned to town for the holidays to gather with old friends. Townie Christmas was by far one of the most popular traditions held at the bar through the years.

Another great holiday tradition that involves Gene's Beer Garden is the annual Morgantown Santa bar crawl. It has included other great Morgantown bars, such as Chestnut Brew Works, Apothecary Ale House, Decker's Creek Yacht

Club, Lefty's Pizza, and 123 Pleasant Street, among others.

The annual Morgantown Santa bar crawl always begins at Gene's.

xxx

Country Road bombs

The 1970s John Denver hit song, "Take Me Home, Country Roads," has become the unofficial state song of West Virginia over the years. It is played at Mountaineer Field and the Coliseum after every WVU victory in football and basketball, respectively. The crowd stays well after the game ends and sings along to the song with the WVU players. Even at Gene's, the song is played on the jukebox, and the patrons loudly sing along after Mountaineer victories. The song is adored by most natives and residents of West Virginia. But there are folks in the state who despise the song because of overplay or of claims the song is actually about Virginia and not West Virginia. One such person used to work at Gene's.

He also liked to ban people from the bar. During one September in the late 1990s, Chris A. and Cheese Plate had been kicked out of the bar for unruly behavior and told never to return. They were devastated with the harsh decision as Cheese Plate lived across the street and Gene's was their favorite place to go. They would watch their friends having the times of their lives inside Gene's from Cheese Plate's living room window. And it was especially hard for Cheese Plate as he was on house arrest. Gene's was the only public place he could go outside his apartment without setting off the tracking signal of his ankle bracelet. It also meant no more cheese plates for him.

Chris and Cheese Plate wanted to take revenge on the cranky bartender. They knew he hated the song "Take Me Home, Country Roads." They would watch from Cheese Plate's apartment. After the sun set when that particular bartender was working, they took turns crawling on their bellies in the dark across Wilson Avenue to Gene's. They would crawl up the front steps, through the side door, and into the back room where the jukebox was located. They would load the jukebox with money and select the John Denver tune dozens of times.

As they crawled out of Gene's, the song would begin to play. The bartender would let it play the first time but after it started a second time, he'd walk to the back room to see who had played the song. There would be no one there. He would skip the song with the jukebox's remote control. The song would start again, and again, and again for most of the night until he would finally pull plug on the jukebox. He would turn it back on when someone wanted to play it. To his disgust, "Take Me Home, Country Roads," would come blaring back on.

This went on for many weeks until the bartender set a trap. After starting one of his shifts, he snuck to the back room and sat down low in a chair by the side door. On his belly, Chris crawled across Wilson Avenue and pushed the door to the back room open. The bartender waited in the chair for him, blocking the path to the jukebox. They stared at each other for a moment until Chris turned his body around and crawled back across the street and disappeared into Cheese Plate's apartment.

Fortunately for Chris and Cheese Plate, that bartender didn't work at Gene's for much longer. They were happily back in the bar, enjoying cheese plates, cold pints of beer, and loud jukebox music. The comforting sound of John Denver's voice played continuously for weeks thereafter in celebration.

A reason not to live above a bar

It was Thursday—a work night. No one can remember the band, but it was a loud, hard-rocking outfit. They had played well past their 11 PM curfew. Sometime a little after midnight, the front door to Gene's busted open.

Grady, who lived upstairs, stormed into the bar, wearing nothing but his tighty whities. He had to work the next morning. His face was red with rage. His wispy gray hair was messed, standing in all directions. He was in bare feet. He was bare chested. He madly approached the band.

"Shut the fuck up!" he screamed at them, before turning to Lucy. "It's about time to cut this shit off!"

He stormed out of the bar.

"I was on my hands and knees behind the bar, laughing," Lucy recalled. "He came in like the wind. No one could get a picture of him. I couldn't stop laughing at him. He was so disheveled and so very pissed off. He looked like Einstein. Oh, Grady was the show that night. No one remembers the band."

Before the band could start their next song, the plug on the PA system was pulled.

Regular local performers at Gene's. Left top, Jamie Lester. Left bottom, Andy Tuck. Center, Gary Antol. Right top, Tom Batchelor. Right bottom, Greg Riordan. Photos Ted Kisko, Heather Kessler.

Popular local acts. Left, bassist Matt Cross. Center top, Dem Donkey Boys. Center bottom, Ryan Cain and the Ables, Right, Ted Kisko and the Sound Situation. Photos Ted Kiso, Heather Kessler.

Popular local acts. Left corner clockwise. Born Again Hindus, Jeff Grable, Brandon Fields, Haley Slagle and the Hardway.

xxx

Gene's Miracle Nation

Former bartender and regular Casey Bicanich understood what Gene's meant to people. When working the bar, he'd often answer the phone, "Hello, you've reached Gene's Miracle Nation."

He was aware enough to know Gene's was the only lifeline for many folks. It was also a place to go if one didn't have anywhere else. For some, it felt like home. Al never hesitated to feed someone who was hungry or give away a pint of beer when one was needed.

Gene's was not only a place that poured beers and served lunch, but it was a place that helped others, especially the people in the neighborhood as well as the Morgantown community. Since Al has owned Gene's, the bar has hosted scores of musical events to help those in need.

Al Bonneroo

For years, Dilip Chandran and I (Jim Antonini) would talk about how Al should have an outdoor music festival in the parking lot behind Gene's. We were convinced he wouldn't be interested. On a hot afternoon in February 2009, the three of us were sitting at the bar at the famous Yo Mama's in New Orleans. We had been somewhat overserved as we each worked on a French Quarter triple-double when Dilip and I proposed to him the idea.

"You know what you ought to do, Al," Dilip said.

"What?"

"You should have a music festival at Gene's."

"Music festival?"

"Outside," I spoke up. "In the parking lot. There's a lot of great original bands in Morgantown. You could sell t-shirts, tickets, and local beer out there. And some of the proceeds could go to charity."

Al took a drink from his bottle of Dixie beer and glanced to the sunny street outside, obviously thinking about the idea.

"We will call it, Al Bonneroo," I said with a laugh.

"Al Bonneroo?" Al chuckled.

"Yeah, like the name of the famous music festival in Tennessee but not quite."

"When?"

"This summer," Dilip said.

"Al Bonneroo," Al said and as we all laughed. "Okay. Let's do it."

The Al Bonneroo music festival has been held five times. It is not affiliated with the Bonnaroo Music Festival in Tennessee in any way. The first two occurred in 2009 and 2010. The first festival in 2009 even had an out-of-town headliner. The fabulous Todd Steed and the Suns of Phere drove all the way from Knoxville, Tennessee, to perform at the first one. Beer from local breweries, like Chestnut Brew Works, and different distributors were served outside. Food trucks and local restaurants, such as Madeleine Marie's, also set up in the parking lot or on the streets surrounding Gene's. The festival was brought back in 2018 and 2019 after a near-decade hiatus. A recently scaled-down version of Al Bonneroo was held in 2023. The festival has always coincided with the Greenmont neighborhood block party that occurs on the last weekend of June every year.

The original idea of Al Bonneroo was to support the neighborhood and community as well as highlight some of Morgantown's finest bands that played original music. Collectively, the five different festivals have raised over $20,000 for various charities, including Pantry Plus and More of Monongalia County, Pack the Bus Preston County, a recovering fund for a neighborhood burn victim, Greenmont Neighborhood Association, and the BOPARC Foundation, among others.

2009 Al Bonneroo
Musical Lineup: Todd Steed and the Suns of Phere, Moon, Come Drinking, Sam Lamont Band, Owen Davis and the Free Hummus All-Stars, Brian Porterfield and the Love Me Knots, The Gear, Jonestown, William Matheny, and Staggering Cardoons
Charity: Recovery Fund for a burn victim in the

neighborhood

2010 Al Bonnero
Musical Lineup: Tom Batchelor Band, Left of the Dial, AC/GREASY, Staggering Cardoons, Brothers Short Band, Sam Lamont Band, 85 Flood, Jonestown, and Born Again Hindus
Charity: Greenmont Neighborhood Preservation Society

2018 Al Bonneroo
Musical Lineup: Owen Davis and the Free Hummus All-Stars, Greg Short, Haley Slagle and the Hardway, The Border States, Phantom Six, Goodwolf, Tom Batchelor Band, Diablo Sandwich, Yellow Dog Union, Kelsie Cannon, Annalies Stealy, and The Jacob's Ferry Stragglers
Charity: Pantry Plus and More of Monongalia County, Pack the Bus Preston County

2019 Al Bonneroo
Musical Lineup: The Greens, Owen Davis and the Free Hummus All-Stars, Bumper Jackson, Born Again Hindus, 18 Strings, Haley Slagle and the Hardway, Before I Sleep, Meadow Run, The Ramps, Sarah Rudy (Hello, June), Kenny West, Davis Kimble, and Will Hutchens

2023 Al Bonneroo
Musical Lineup: Helicopter Collective, Ponderosa, Hale Slagle and the Hardway, Sister

Tall, Grace Campbell and Dalton Matheny, Ted Kisko, and Schnell and Paris
Charity: BOPARC Foundation

Images from the first Al Bonneroo in 2009, featuring Brian Porterfield and the Love Me Knots.

Lennon thing

Images from the annual Lennon Thing charity event at Gene's.

Over the past five years, Gene's has held a live music event on December 8 to celebrate the life and music of John Lennon on the anniversary of his death. It is one of the most popular events regularly held at Gene's. Like Al Bonneroo, one of the main goals of the Lennon Thing was to raise money for local charities. Nearly $15,000 has been raised through the years for such charities as Empty Bowls of Monongalia County, The Miracle League, and Stepping Stones. Because of its popularity, the Lennon Thing 5 held this past December, in 2023, was changed from a one-night to a two-night event.

xxx

Art, art, and more art

Along with the vibrant music scene, Gene's has been an inspiration for many local artists in the Morgantown area. The bar's inside and outside walls and ceilings have been decorated with paintings, wood sculptures, drawings, stained glass, and murals.

Also, several artist exhibitions have been held at Gene's through the years. One exhibition displayed photographs of actual buttholes of different people from the neighborhood. Al thought it best to move that exhibit to the pool room in the basement—a more discrete location than the bar area, where people were eating and drinking.

In the early 1990s, local artist Robin Dallas did
different sketches of the inside and outside of
Gene's. Al sold these sketches for years. They are
still available for purchase.

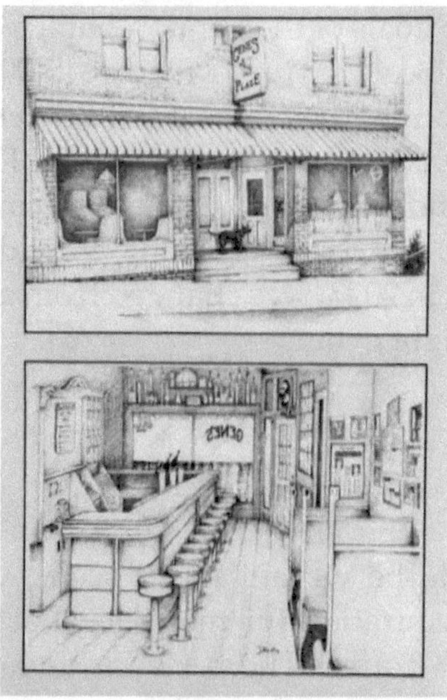

Sketches of the outside and inside of Gene's by Robin
Dallas.

Soon after, artisan and bar regular Mike Roh
completed the iconic hot dog and beer stained-
glass window that lights the bar to this day (see
front cover of this book). The famous traveling
troubadour, songwriter, and former preacher
Abe Partridge once remarked during a
performance at Gene's, "That's got to be the only
hot dog ever put on a stained-glass window."

Al after being gifted the Gene's stained-glass window.

As mentioned before, Mike was also responsible for the wood carving of the outline of the state of West Virginia that hangs on the back wall of the stage at Gene's.

Photo of the Gene's stage in back with the West Virginia state carving.

During the renovations of the back room of Gene's during the *Covid* pandemic, local artist Jessie Haring spent several days and nights on her back on top of scaffolding. In homage to Italian painter Michelangelo, she painted what is referred to as the *Sis 'Gene's' Chapel* on the ceiling in front of the bar's restrooms.

The *Sis 'Gene's' Chapel* in progress by artist local Jessie Haring.

As a tribute to the glorious history of Gene's Beer Garden and its founders, prolific artist and bar regular Brian Pickens painted a mural on an outside wall of the building next to the bar (see back cover of this book). The vibrant mural features members of the first family of Gene's, Joe and Gene Perilli. It also cleverly included a snowmobile in reference to the one Brian Reed drove through a snowstorm from Grafton to Morgantown just to drink a beer at Gene's.

The Gene's Mural in progress with artist Brian Pickens.

More recently, the great Liz Pavlovic, a devoted regular at Gene's and hot dog aficionado created wonderful new stickers for the bar.

Gene's stickers created by artist Liz Pavlovic.

Chapter 7
Morgantown's Original Sports Bar

Sports were put here to break our hearts. And that's been true of our local teams, who we've watched suffer great defeats through the years. And we endured them all at Gene's.

There was the 13-9 WVU football loss to the awful and offensively challenged Pitt Panthers in 2007. All-American Pat McAfee missed two short field goals and star quarterback Pat White left the game early due to injury. With a win in that game, WVU (arguably, the greatest team in school history) would have played for the NCAA College Football National Championship in New Orleans against an overrated Ohio State team.

We watched coach Bob Huggins console his star forward and leading scorer Da'Sean Butler who blew out his knee during the Mountaineers comeback against the hated Duke Blue Devils in the in the second half of the 2010 NCAA College Basketball Final Four. Without Butler, the comeback faded. The basketball team hasn't really challenged on the national level since.

There was Gold Glove Pittsburgh Pirate second baseman Chico Lind who made an unlikely but crucial error on a routine groundball in the ninth inning of the last game of the National League Championship in 1992 against the Atlanta Braves. The winner of the game would advance to the World Series. The Braves slow-footed first baseman Sid Bream would later plod home that inning with the winning run, scoring just ahead of a lily-armed throw to the plate from Pirate outfielder Barry Bonds. Gene's regular, Dave Snedeker was quoted as saying after the game, "It was the first time I put the gun all the way in my mouth."

The Pittsburgh Steelers lost to the hated Dallas Cowboys in Super Bowl XXX. Steeler QB Neil O'Donnell was dreadful, tossing two soul-crushing second half interceptions directly into the arms of a mediocre Cowboy defensive back. The Super Bowl loss was bad enough, but Al also lost the front window of Gene's that night when one of the regulars fell through it (more on that later in this chapter).

And there were so many more. WVU couldn't get a rebound and squandered a 19-point lead in the last three minutes of the NCAA basketball quarterfinals for a chance to advance to the 2005 Final Four against Louisville. The loss to Notre Dame in the Fiesta Bowl in 1989 when star quarterback Major Harris got hurt on the third play of the game. The Pittsburgh Steelers laid an egg in Super Bowl XLV against the Green Bay Packers. The Pirates failed to advance through the playoffs to make the World Series in 1990, 1991, 1992, 2013, 2014, and 2015. And we could go on. . . .

Despite all the disappointing results, there have been some great victories through the years as well. Pat White, Steve Slaton, and Owen Schmidt led the Mountaineer football team to dominant wins in the Sugar Bowl in 2006 over Georgia and in the Fiesta Bowl in 2008 over Oklahoma. Da'Sean Butler hit a dramatic, last second three-point shot to defeat mighty Georgetown in the 2010 Big East Championship.

And we can't forget when Darren Studstill tossed a touchdown pass to Eddie Hill in the closing seconds against Boston College to finish the 1993 season undefeated and earn a trip to the Sugar Bowl. The wild celebration at Gene's that night spread from the bar through Sunnyside and eventually ended at the Mountaineer Stadium as several drunk regulars welcomed the team home from Boston as the sun came up.

There was the magical, undefeated run by the Mountaineer football team in 1988 led by Major Harris. And probably the best of all, the Pirates defeated the Cincinnati Reds in the 2013 National League wildcard game as the fans serenaded the Reds' losing pitcher Johnny Cueto. The constant chants of 'QUAY-TOE' 'QUAY-TOE' 'QUAY-TOE' could be heard for hours reverberating through the Greenmont night.

xxx

Hot Rod Hundley and Jerry West

Hot Rod Hundley played for the WVU basketball team from 1954-1957. He scored over 2,000 points, was a two-time All-American, and still holds eight school records. He was most remembered during his college days for his on-court, in-game antics—shooting hooks from the free throw line, spinning the ball on his finger, and dribbling and passing behind his back. He was the first player taken in the NBA draft in 1957. He probably became the most famous for being the long-time radio and television voice of the Utah Jazz.

Hundley returned to Gene's for a visit in early 2010 when his number was being retired by WVU. Al let him guest-bartend at Gene's the night before his jersey retirement ceremony.

"When someone would pay him for their drink," Al recalled. "Rod would put the money in his pocket instead of the cash register."

Both Al and Gene's are featured in the documentary about Hundley's life, *Hot Rod The Documentary, the Untold Story of Hot Rod Hundley.*

Hot Rod Hundley guest-bartending at Gene's in 2010.

Jerry West is the most famous person to be associated with West Virginia sports. West played basketball at WVU from 1956-1960 and led the Mountaineers to the national championship game his senior season. He was an All-American for multiple seasons, is the all-time leading scorer and rebounder at WVU, and holds twelve school records. He won a gold medal for the USA in basketball at the 1960 summer Olympics in Rome. After college, West went on to become an NBA legend playing for the Los Angeles Lakers. He was inducted into the Naismith Basketball Hall of Fame in 1980 and was the model for the current logo of the NBA.

There are photographs, one of which still hangs on the wall in the bar, of West eating a hot dog in Gene's after his WVU playing career was over. There also was a handmade sign that hung for years on the walls at Gene's that read, "Welcome Back, Jerry West." The sign was made for when he returned to play in an NBA exhibition game at the Coliseum against the New York Knicks in the early 1970s. The sign currently hangs in the Speakeasy in the basement of Gene's.

Jerry West enjoying hot dogs with friends and family on a visit to Gene's.

xxx

Do I still get a free beer?

Gene's softball teams through the years.

One of the last softball teams sponsored by Gene's had a hyperactive and overly enthusiastic third baseman named Richie. He fielded warm-up balls rolled to him like it was the last inning of the World Series. He fired them one after another like bullets across the infield diamond, continually stinging the gloved hand of first basemen Gary Davies.

This was all well and good, but the Gene's pitcher at the time was the bear of a man Big Bob Hamilton who stood six feet, six inches tall and weighed over two-hundred-and-fifty pounds. Being so tall and wide, Bob was a significant barrier between first and third base as Richie zipped the warmup balls back and forth between the two bases. Bob's height indeed proved to be a problem as one of the thrown balls beaned him in the side of the head. The sound was nauseating. It sounded like someone violently striking a watermelon with one hard swing of a baseball bat. Bob instantly collapsed onto the dusty pitcher's mound. Blood dripped from his ear.

Woozy, he was helped off the field by several teammates and taken out of the lineup for that night's game. Sometime around the third inning as he sat on the bench, Bob appeared confused but serious as he stared to the diamond and asked, "Why am I not playing tonight?"

"Because you got hit in the head."

"I did? When?"

"You don't remember getting hit by Richie?"

"No."

"We better get him to a hospital."

As was custom, Gene's softball players were each gifted at least one (oftentimes more) free beer by Al after every game. After that particular game, as the Gene's softball team celebrated into the night, the bar's phone rang. It was Bob. He was calling from an examination room at the hospital. One of the emergency room doctors had given him permission to make the call.

"Hey, Al," he said. "The doc says I may get to leave once they get the results of the MRI on my head."

"How do you feel?" Al inquired.

"Do I still get my free beer tonight?" he asked, ignoring Al's question. "Even though I didn't play."

xxx

The cheapest beer in the world

Through the years, Gene's hosted parties for important sporting events, such as the Super Bowl and WVU football bowl games. Al would buy pizza and chicken wings. The regulars would often bring their favorite covered dishes and snacks.

WVU was playing Texas A&M in the Liberty Bowl in 2014. Al had purchased dozens of pizzas and buckets of chicken wings that covered multiple tables in the back room of the bar.

An earnest young man, who shall not be named, entered Gene's with a group of friends. He studied the many taps of beer, before wandering over to the cooler and checking out the bottle and can selections. Unable to decide, he approached Al, who was behind the bar.

"Do you have any specials today?" he innocently asked.

"Yeah," Al bluntly responded. "We have cheap beer and free food in the back. I'd say that's pretty fucking special!"

There are not too many places in the world where you can get a can of Black Label beer for $1. And there can't be anywhere else where you can get a 24-ounce can of Pabst Blue Ribbon for $2.50.

xxx

Neil O'Donnell versus Gene's front window

A view of Gene's front window from inside. Photo by Ted Kisko.

It was late in the fourth quarter of Super Bowl XXX. The despised Dallas Cowboys were about to beat the Pittsburgh Steelers to become World Champions. Gene's was packed. Most of the people were drunk and had been since the start of the game. The crowd that night was about 95% in favor of their beloved Steelers with 1% for the Cowboys. The other 4% there didn't give a damn about the game. They were only there for the party. As the Cowboys ran out the clock towards victory, the mood in Gene's had quickly changed from festive and optimistic to angry and sour.

Tom Dunham and Roadie, both drunk and ornery, had been acting up for most of the second half. Al was ready to kick them both out of the bar when an overserved and unsteady Dave Weston, who was returning from the bathroom, tripped on the floor mat that ran behind the barstools. Being a rather big man, he couldn't gather himself to regain his balance. His momentum dragged his heavy body forward in direct line with the front plate glass window of Gene's.

With his arms flailing, he forcefully crashed headfirst into the window, breaking the three-inch thick glass into several pieces. He was stuck with the upper half of his body outside the bar and the lower half still inside. As his body precariously rested on the windowpane, a large triangular piece of jagged glass hung over him like a guillotine.

Al and Jim Bob, who was bartending at the

time, rushed outside to the sidewalk in front of the bar to check on Weston. Miraculously, there was not one drop of blood.

"Quick, call 9-1-1!" Al ordered as someone inside called, "And don't touch him or that piece of glass hanging over him!"

Al and Jim Bob continued to examine Weston to make sure his forehead that went through the window and his gut that rested on the broken glass of the windowpane weren't cut open. They didn't let him move and tried to keep him calm as they waited for an ambulance.

A guy everyone at Gene's called Too Tall had been drinking during the game at one of barstools next to the front window. Ignoring Al's order to not touch the large piece of broken glass that dangled over Weston, he grabbed it, thinking he would stabilize it. Instead, the thick piece of glass snapped from the top window seal that held it in place. The piece of glass fell outward and landed directly on Al, Jim Bob, and Dave Weston, smashing into hundreds of pieces.

"Jesus Christ, Too Tall!" Al hollered as he quickly brushed the broken pieces of glass from his hair and checked to see if he'd been cut. "What did I tell you?"

The ambulance roared up. The paramedics hopped out and examined the situation. They didn't want to move Weston in case his belly had been stabbed open.

"You're doing a good job," they kept telling

him. "Stay still. You're doing great."

Eventually, the two paramedics lifted Weston's body away from the shattered window and pulled him inside the bar. Unbelievably, he only had one cut—a thin nick on top of his forehead.

Not getting any attention because of the broken front window ordeal, Roadie suddenly punched the back of the beer tap system. The force knocked all the beer taps open, causing beer to flow uncontrollably all over the floor behind the bar.

"Get out!" Al screamed at Roadie, before glancing at Tom Dunham. "And you, too!"

"Me, too?" Tom asked.

"Yeah, you too!"

"What'd I do?"

"Guilt by association! Now get out!"

Tom Dunham and Roadie

Thanks, Bob Huggins!

Mike Roh, Pat Brezito, Al, and I said we would get our heads shaved on the stage at Gene's if the WVU basketball team ever made it to the Final Four in the NCAA March Madness tournament. We also agreed that hair-styling legend and local gadabout John Cale would be the one who would shave our heads.

This pact was made before basketball coaching legend and future hall-of-famer Bob Huggins was hired by WVU. After his hiring, we knew our full heads of hair were doomed. It didn't take long for Huggins to accomplish the feat. He was hired before the 2007-2008 season and had WVU in the Final Four in 2010. Unfortunately, WVU lost to Duke in the Final Four semifinals by the score of 78-57, and we lost our hair on the stage of Gene's in front of a packed house. No one enjoyed the spectacle more than John Cale.

Head shaving by John Cale with before and after
photos. Photos by Jenny Roberts.

xxx

"It was the best of times, it was the worst of times,
it was the age of wisdom, it was the age of
foolishness."

—Charles Dickens

It was the summer of 2001. The television cable
company in Morgantown would show the live
broadcast of the Pittsburgh Pirates game at its
scheduled time each night on a local sports
channel. Because of a lack of interesting content,
the channel would re-broadcast a tape of the

game later that same evening. I would often meet up with Ryan Nicholson that summer to watch the Pirates as we loved baseball, and the Pirates were our favorite team.

The Pirates were awful at the time (and still are, as of this writing). The franchise was in the middle of what would become a nearly unfathomable 20-year losing season streak that would not end until nine years later, in 2013. So, on most nights that summer, we'd watch the Pirates lose. Despite the dreadful nightly performance by our beloved Buccos, we often would hang out at Gene's late enough to catch the re-broadcast of the game we'd watched earlier in the evening. But at one point in the evening, after having consumed several beers, we were more than a little tipsy.

In the second watching of the game, we would be more boisterous, cheering more enthusiastically and yelling encouragement to the beleaguered Pirates at the TV, hoping in some stupid way to change the outcome of the game already played. Others also would join in on the loud cheering, not knowing it was a tape of a losing game that had ended hours before. It all sounds so ridiculous now, and it was. Also, during that summer, the local beer distributor had trouble acquiring Pabst Blue Ribbon beer, one of the most popular and affordable beers served at Gene's and our beer of choice at the time. We fondly look back to that summer and refer to it as The Summer of the Great PBR Famine. It seemed that summer would never end, and the Pirates would go on to lose more than two hundred games.

xxx

The thrill of victory and the agony of defeat — The Gene's Olympics

Once when Al was away on vacation, two former Gene's bartenders, Shey and Ashley Greene, wanted to inject some excitement into the bar. It was early August—the dog days of summer. The place was dead. Everyone was bored. They came up with the idea of having the first (and only) Gene's Olympics.

There were three events. Those who wanted to participate had to pay a $25 entry fee. The first event was a relay race that involved a three-person team. The first person had to chug a beer. After the beer was completely consumed, the second member of the team had to eat an entire cheese plate by themselves. After that, the third person had to eat a hot dog with chili, onions, and mustard. The first team to finish all three parts of the relay was the winner. The folks at the bar who watched the event felt sorry for the poor person who had to choke down an entire cheese plate. It wasn't pretty.

The second event of the Gene's Olympics was

139

another relay in which a two-person team chugged from the same pitcher of beer using straws. The third and final event, the most messy, was a one-person challenge to see who could eat the most Gene's wieners (no bun) in one sitting. As it turned out, the winner ended up consuming an amazing twenty-eight wieners in fifteen minutes. He disappeared soon after the event and wasn't seen for days.

At the end of the Gene's Olympics, there was an actual ceremony on the stage in which medals were awarded to the winners. Instead of the national anthem, "Take Me Home, Country Roads" was played on the jukebox.

Al was not too happy about the unsanctioned event when he saw action photos on Facebook of the different Gene's Olympians competing in his bar. He claimed to have lost a lot of money that day. Shey swore he didn't. But thinking back to the event, he probably did. Unfortunately, none of the medalists of the different events wanted their names included in the publication of this book.

Fun Run for Special Olympics

Clockwise from right top corner, Shey and her dogs; bottom, David Foreman, Tom Bloom, and Mark Tinsley compete in the Gene's Run.

For thirty years, Gene's sponsored and hosted a 4-mile Fun Run and Walk through the Greenmont, South Park, and First Ward neighborhoods. The last Gene's Run was held in 2016. The event took place on the first Sunday of every August, usually (but not intentionally) on one of the hottest days of the summer. Hundreds of runners would participate each year. A large tent would be set up in the parking lot behind Gene's, and participants would be permitted to enjoy free beer long into the night after the run. Al estimated that well over $50,000 was raised through the years for the local Special Olympics charity.

xxx

Road trips

Road trips to Pittsburgh had always been popular with Al and the folks who hung out at Gene's. There were countless trips to Pirate opening days and WVU football games against their bitter rival, the Pitt Panthers. The Pirate games usually included a small group of Gene's regulars who Al would take to Pittsburgh in his van.

The road trips to WVU-Pitt football games were a whole different animal. A bus (sometimes two) would be chartered to transport a large group from Gene's. These trips could get ugly, especially when it was time to head back to Morgantown. There was always too much beer, rum, and whiskey. There were lost wallets, phones, and coats. There would be people missing and people passed out. There were fights. There were keg stands on the bus. Spilled stomach contents everywhere. It also has been rumored that one young fellow drunkenly lost his virginity in the back of the bus on a return trip home to Morgantown. There was at least one arrest. One Gene's regular was arrested outside of Heinz Field after a glorious WVU victory for assaulting an officer. He had slapped a Pittsburgh city police horse in the ass. Owen Davis nearly drowned in the blue sanitized toilet water from the bus bathroom on one trip. While urinating, the bus driver had to slam on his brakes when going through the Fort Pitt tunnel.

"All I recall was a big blue wave splashing over me," Owen remembered.

Captain Morgan — don't leave home without him

The beer drinking started at 8 AM at Gene's. Al had chartered a bus to take a group from Gene's to watch the WVU football team battle their hated rival, the Pitt Panthers, at Heinz Field. The bus arrived at the bar at 9 AM. A keg was quickly loaded onto the bus. It took about two hours to get from Morgantown to Pittsburgh. Two more hours of beer drinking, as well as whiskey shots, was just enough time to get the Gene's crew ready for their big day in Pittsburgh.

The bus reached Pittsburgh and parked at Station Square. They chose to park there as the area has many bars and restaurants to get a drink or a bite to eat before the game. The group would later take a boat shuttle from there across the Allegheny River to the stadium.

Houlihan's sports bar had been open for exactly one minute before about sixty drunk, rowdy, and horned-up Gene's regulars poured in at 11:01 AM. The boisterous invaders from Morgantown blew past the speechless young lady hostess at the entrance, and all sixty regulars headed straight for the bar. None of them were there for food. They wanted more alcohol—a *lot* more alcohol. The expressions on the faces of the two bartenders were one part repulsion and another part horror. It would end up being a long afternoon for them. Kickoff was still four hours away.

Being the biggest, and drunkest, member of the Gene's group, Mike Moran, all six foot six and three hundred and eighty pounds of him, led the way. Charles Randolph trailed close behind him. Charles and Mike were both bartending at Gene's at the time, and they both lived in apartments above the bar. They were inseparable.

"I'll take a quadruple rum and coke," Moran said, before motioning to Charles. "And he'll have a triple rum and coke."

With a roll of her eyes, the bartender stepped away to make the drinks for Moran and Charles as the others from the Gene's crew yelled out drink orders of their own. The bartender returned with two pint glasses of mostly clear liquor drinks on ice. There couldn't have been more than a drop or two of coke in each glass. She set the drinks on the bar in front of Moran.

"Which one is the triple," Moran asked in his high squeaky voice without hesitation, looking concerned, "and which one is the quadruple?"

"Does it even matter at this point?" the bartender answered.

"Yeah," Moran squawked, pulling a pint bottle of Captain Morgan rum from his coat pocket, and adding more rum to each glass until they overflowed onto the bar. "I don't wanna get shortchanged!"

After a couple of hours at Houlihan's, somehow everyone from Gene's had boarded one of the boats of the Gateway Clipper Fleet and made it across the river to Heinz Field in time for kickoff.

As the sun set late that day, the game was but a blur for most of the crew from Gene's. WVU clung to a seven-point lead over the Pitt Panthers, who had the ball on the 14-yard line and were ready to score in the waning seconds of the game. A frosty wind suddenly had stiffened off the Allegheny River. Large flakes of snow poured from the dark November sky and swirled with the howling wind through the stadium.

It was fourth down—the last play of the game. With a fierce rush from the Mountaineer defensive line, Pitt quarterback Rod Rutherford desperately flung a lifeless lame duck of a pass into the stiff snowy wind. The ball harmlessly floated to ground incomplete, sealing the victory for the Mountaineers. The jubilant and inebriated members of the Gene's crew danced and partied in the stands of Heinz Field until forced to leave by stadium security.

The brass sound of "Take Me Home, Country Roads" filled the air along the banks of the three rivers that formed the city. The Pittsburgh Sax Man, his saxophone case overflowing with $10 and $20 bills—entirely donated by WVU fans—

played the Mountaineer victory song on repeat late into the night as thousands of giddy Mountaineer fans flowed from the stadium.

Back to the river shuttle, the entire Gene's crew was forced to board the Good Ship Lollipop, the smallest boat of the Gateway Clipper fleet. The candy-themed boat was originally used to give young children riverboat tours of the city of Pittsburgh. After the Gene's crew loaded the cramped boat, Randy "The Wiz" Nieman took his position at the bow as the boat pushed away from the riverbank and set sail across the Allegheny to Station Square. The Wiz's long, wavy gray hair danced with the stiff wind that blew in his face. Folding his arms across his chest and bending his knee to place his right foot on the rail of the bow of the boat, he resembled George Washington crossing the Potomac. The Wiz wore a confident smirk, like the one Washington likely wore when knew he was about to kick some British ass.

It was a quiet and sleepy two-hour bus ride to Morgantown. Once back, the entire Gene's crew, except for two members — one lost and one arrested — entered the bar to a rousing ovation, like heroes returning from battle. That day is still referred to as Victory in Pittsburgh Day. Most everyone enjoyed another beer or two, before scattering into the night, only to return to Gene's early the next day. As he was leaving the bar, the Wiz grinned, "It's good to be home, man. It's good to be fuckin' home."

Left, Gene's crew loaded on the bus to Pittsburgh. Right, Charles and Moran in Houlihan's. Photos by Jenny Roberts

What did you do to Peanut?

It was opening day for the Pittsburgh Pirates when they still played at Three Rivers Stadium. Al took his van from Gene's to the game. Brian Jones, Reed Davis, Ben Mackey, Peanut, and maybe a couple of others joined. Reed and Peanut had been drinking all morning at Gene's before they left and kept drinking for the entire 70-mile ride to Pittsburgh. When they left Morgantown, Peanut only had $3 in his pocket.

It was just the first inning, and Reed and Peanut were already wasted. Al asked Ben, who was a city cop at the time, if he had his handcuffs. He did. Al joked he should handcuff Reed and Peanut to their seats, so they wouldn't lose them.

During the third inning, Al ran up to the concession stand to get something to eat. On his way back to the seats, he saw Peanut staggering up the stairs towards him. Al asked if he knew where he was going and if he could find his way back to the seats. Peanut nodded and pulled his ticket from the pocket of his shorts, showing it to Al.

Well, as Al predicted, Peanut disappeared. He never came back to his seat. The game ended. Al and the others headed out of the stadium to the parking lot. They didn't know what to do. They had a few beers by the van and waited to see if he'd show up. It soon became dark and was getting late. They decided to go to the old Clark Bar and Grill that used to be near the stadium to have a nightcap and grab something to eat. They returned an hour or two later to the van—still, no Peanut. They decided to drive back to Morgantown. It seemed like a long ride home. No one in the van said much. It was late when they got back to the bar. Al opened the door.

"What'd you do to Peanut?" Pam, the bartender at the time, asked.

"We lost him," Al said.

"Lost him?"

"He wandered off."

"Well, the Pittsburgh police have him now. Here's the number. You need to go get him."

"I can't drive back up there now."

So, Al called the number. He spoke to a lady cop named Mary. He asked if Peanut had been arrested. She said no. A patrol car picked him up on the North side of Pittsburgh not far from the stadium. When the police picked him up, they said, "Boy, I wouldn't be walkin' alone on these streets at this time of night."

So, the police brought him to the downtown station. She asked Al if he could come get him. Al told her he couldn't, but if she could put him up in a hotel for the night, he'd pick him up in the morning and pay her for the room.

After an initial reluctance, Officer Mary agreed to find Peanut lodging for the night. She drove him to the Knight's Inn hotel in Bridgeville, a suburb of Pittsburgh not far from where she lived. As they neared the hotel, Peanut asked if she could stop and buy him a six-pack of beer. He told her he didn't have any money but assured her that Al would pay her back. She stopped and bought him the beer. Finally, at the hotel after getting checked in, Peanut asked her if she wanted to come into the room and have a beer with him. They ended up having more than beer. She spent the night with him at the hotel.

Al called Officer Mary the next morning to arrange to pay for Peanut's room.

"No worries," she told Al. "The room's on me. We had a great time together last night. Blaine is a wonderful man."

She left him in the room. Peanut kissed her goodbye, showered, walked a short way to Interstate 79, and hitched a ride with a WVU college student who was headed to Morgantown. As they neared the West Virginia state line, Peanut told the kid to stop at the Mt. Morris,

Pennsylvania, exit off the interstate.

"I never pass Abe's Place without stopping in," he said to the kid as he hopped out of the car.

Peanut walked a mile and entered the smoky tavern. Little did he know, there was a man sitting at the bar who owed him $50. He paid Peanut and bought him several beers, before driving him to Morgantown and dropping him off at Gene's.

Peanut strutted into Gene's to a rousing cheer. He walked with a swagger like he was the most important person in the world—the King of Greenmont. He felt bigger than God. Not only was he buzzed that morning on free beers, but he was $50 richer than he had been the day before and had given a lady cop from Pittsburgh the ride of her life.

Chapter 8
Last Call

If this was an audiobook, this would be the time when Lucy would loudly, but with as much love as possible at two in the morning, announce "Last call!" like she does several nights a week.

"I have a hard time saying no," she said when it came to closing the bar at the end of the night. "Some of those kids in here late have just gotten off work at the bars and restaurants downtown. They just want to have a little fun after work. I know, I've been there."

Left, Al and Julie. Right, Al with his kids at Gene's, Julianna, Kirby, and Lindsay.

Here is one last story to end the book.

Happy Father's Day

Adrian Rawle was a young man who was mostly homeless. He was recognizable around the neighborhood as he wore his hair in long dreadlocks, and his pants were always ripped. He'd been undergoing treatment for a variety of mental illnesses he was struggling to control. Al used to let him come into Gene's and would feed him hot dogs and pepperoni rolls and let him drink beers in the back room for free if he didn't bother anyone. Al also would load the jukebox full of credits. Adrian loved to play the Motley Crue song, "Girls, Girls, Girls" over and over. When it was bitterly cold outside, Al would let him sleep in the upstairs hallway between the apartments above the bar.

Al also would occasionally buy him new pairs of pants when the ones he wore were too torn and tattered. On one Father's Day months before Adrian would die, he gave Al a small gift and a Father's Day card. Even in Adrian's frazzled mental state, Al's generosity was not unappreciated. For Adrian and so many others through the years, Gene's has been a lighthouse that has provided warmth and friendship.

During one late night, a group of Gene's regulars were in the back room playing jukebox music and giving toasts about what they were grateful for. Adrian usually didn't say much or interact with anyone when he was at Gene's. But on that night, he spoke up, asking if he could give a toast. He raised his glass and said two simple sentences.

"We're all here! Let's drink some beer!
Adrian Rawle, 2016. RIP.

Here's to another eighty years at Gene's!

In the infamous words of longtime Gene's bartender, Steve Brady,

"We're gonna live forever!"

Acknowledgments

This book would not have been possible without stories and photos sent to us from many people, especially Lucy, Josh, Shey, Tarik, and Laurel Jones. Extra special thanks go to Jenny Roberts for many of the older photos and Ted Kisko for much of the new photography with help from Ashley Hemm included in the book. We greatly appreciate Jon Vehse for the title suggestion. Thanks also go to the expert editing job performed by Geoffrey Fuller who lives just a few short blocks from Gene's.

About the Authors

Al **Bonner** is the current owner of Gene's Beer Garden and, in his words, "kept the lights on and the beer flowing" since 1985. He is a lifelong resident of the Greenmont neighborhood in Morgantown, West Virginia. Check out his Gene's website: https://genesbeergarden.com for Gene's-related merchandise, blogs, podcasts, and event updates.

Jim Antonini got his first hair cut at Gene's when he was three years old. He spent many evenings there during his graduate school days at WVU in the 1990s when he lived a block away from the bar. He is an award-winning author from West Virginia who has had three novels published by Pump Fake Press: *Bullets for Silverware*, a gritty, murder-mystery thriller set in the backwoods of West Virginia and a finalist for the Appodlachia 2020 Best Appalachian Book of the Year; *Like Falling from an Airplane* is a romantic, urban drama set on the downtown streets and back alleys of San Francisco; *Wild Bill Rides Again* is about a socially awkward middle-aged family man who steals one million dollars and goes on an unforgettable joyride across the country. His books and other Pump Fake Press merchandise are available at https://jimantonini.com